THE LITTLE FREE LIBRARY BOOK

MARGRET ALDRICH

COFFEE HOUSE PRESS • 2015

COPYRIGHT © 2015 Margret Aldrich
COVER AND BOOK DESIGN Linda Koutsky
AUTHOR PHOTOGRAPH © Nathan Kavlie

Coffee House Press books are available to the trade through our primary distributor, Consortium Book Sales & Distribution, cbsd.com or (800) 283-3572. For personal orders, catalogs, or other information, write to: info@coffeehousepress.org.

Coffee House Press is a nonprofit literary publishing house. Support from private foundations, corporate giving programs, government programs, and generous individuals helps make the publication of our books possible. We gratefully acknowledge their support in detail in the back of this book.

Visit us at coffeehousepress.org.

LIBRARY OF CONGRESS CIP INFORMATION

Aldrich, Margret, 1975–
The little free library book / Margret Aldrich.
   pages cm. — (Books in action)
ISBN 978-1-56689-407-4 (hardback)
1. Small libraries.   2. Libraries and community.   3. Reading promotion.
   4. Free material.   5. Do-it-yourself work.   6. Handicraft.
I. Title.
Z675.S57A43 2015
027—dc23

PRINTED IN THE UNITED STATES

To Little Free Library
patrons and stewards
everywhere.

CONTENTS

"To build up a library
is to create a life.
It's never just a random
collection of books."

—CARLOS MARÍA DOMÍNGUEZ

FOREWORD
A SWEETER SIDE OF HUMANITY

I originally started Little Free Library because of the sheer delight I saw when people approached a Little Free Library for the first time. Now, four years and more than twenty-five thousand Little Free Libraries later, my first observation has held true: humanity's sweeter side emerges when neighbors share books and ideas.

Little Free Library has been called a global literacy movement, a revolution in neighborhood conversation, and the best media exchange of the year. As tens of thousands of stewards and users continue to reimagine what a Little Free Library can do and be, their creativity and insight guide us toward greater heights and a more collaborative global community.

Little Free Libraries and Literacy

There are more than eleven thousand small towns across the United States that don't have a public library. While this might seem like a daunting obstacle to tackle, Rotary Clubs, Lions, 4-H groups, Boy and Girl Scout troops, churches, schools, businesses, and many other groups and individuals are stepping up to take care of their country and make sure *all* small towns have a Little Free Library and free access to books.

Little Free Libraries can also help address community issues around literacy. In Ohio, a new law states that third graders cannot advance to fourth grade unless they meet minimum reading standards. In Cleveland, an estimated 75 percent of third-graders aren't expected to meet this requirement. The

community calls this their literacy tsunami. Will significant government support and funds be available to address this problem? While we hope so, we suspect there will not be anything close to adequate funding to meet this challenge.

How can this situation in Cleveland, which is also occurring in many other communities across the country, be alleviated? To me, this question isn't so much about solving problems on a national or global scale, but about caring for and improving individual neighborhoods. Can you and your neighbors step up and take responsibility for the houses next to you? Can you solve literacy concerns on your block or street?

Together with a variety of organizations and individuals, Little Free Library is helping neighborhoods that are dedicated to supporting literacy. I am truly convinced Little Free Library stewards are the best people for this kind of work. They are the perfect concerned citizens, ready to pick up the charge, improve their neighborhoods, and ensure that all their neighbors read well and often.

The Little Free Library Book

Over the years, we've been asked many times by friends across the country and around the world to tell the tale of our grassroots literacy efforts. To that end, we've worked with author Margret Aldrich and nonprofit publisher Coffee House Press to create the book you now hold in your hands. While there are many reasons to write a book, I think that telling the story of how we work together as neighbors to make our world a better place is about as good as it gets.

In the following pages, you'll learn about the story of Little Free Library as told through the heartwarming accounts of our stewards. We believe that together we are greater than the sum of our parts, and that by sharing our stories, we can better address the issues that affect each and every one of us around the world.

It has been said that love is based on serving each other, and this is what is happening every time another simple little box on a post gets erected. With nearly a thousand new Little Free Libraries going up every month, Little Free Library is spreading unprecedented growth, and yes, love, aimed at a common cause. As stronger community connections form around free book sharing, the sweeter side of our shared humanity will expand like ripples across a pond.

—Todd Bol, Creator, Executive Director, and First Steward of Little Free Library

INTRODUCTION

It all started with a sign that read "Free Books." Todd Bol built the first Little Free Library for his Hudson, Wisconsin, front yard in 2009 as a tribute to his mother, a former teacher and lifelong reader. Today that single, small idea has grown into a cultural phenomenon: There are more than twenty-five thousand Little Free Libraries worldwide—spread across all fifty states and more than eighty countries—and dozens more are established every week.

The concept is simple: A Little Free Library is a box of books, posted in an accessible spot, often in a residential yard near a sidewalk. Everyone who passes by is welcome to stop and browse the books that fill the microlibrary. See something you like? Take it home. Have a book to share? Add it to the mix. Because the charming book exchanges run on this "take a book, return a book" honor system, the inventory constantly changes, and they offer something for every reader—from gardening guides to Russian novels to picture books.

Beyond promoting literacy and a love of reading, a Little Free Library—LFL in shorthand—sparks a feeling of community, too. When people pause to flip through the hardcovers and paperbacks, they are just as likely to strike up a conversation with their neighbor as they are to find their next great read. Little Free Libraries help make blocks friendlier and more connected, and the best of them become the neighborhood watercooler—an informal meeting spot that acts as a small social anchor in the community.

"The reason Little Free Library has been successful is that people tell us, constantly, 'I've met more neighbors in a week than I've met in thirty years,'" says Bol. "It engages and brings neighborhoods together, and folks talk to each other more than they ever have."

In 2010, after Bol had seen the first Little Free Library strike a chord with his neighbors, he teamed with Rick Brooks, a community-minded outreach program manager at the University of Wisconsin–Madison, to think about how they could share the tiny Libraries with the rest of the world. They decided to start with a big goal: to build 2,510 libraries—one more than Andrew Carnegie.

The steel-tycoon-turned-philanthropist was a fitting role model for Bol and Brooks's Little Free Library project. Carnegie had grown up a poor Scottish American immigrant intent on improving himself, but he had limited access to books. As a teenaged textile-mill worker, he couldn't afford the two-dollar subscription fee to his local library, so he wrote them a letter asking for the fee to be waived. The request was flatly denied—until the *Pittsburgh Dispatch* printed the letter. (Even a nineteenth-century library didn't want bad press.) Books became stepping-stones to Carnegie's future success, and he never forgot it. After rising to wealth, he made sure that people of all ages, classes, and ethnic heritages would have free access to books and a similar chance to improve their futures. Between 1883 and 1929, Carnegie dedicated his fortune to building public libraries—2,509 of them—from the United States, Canada, and Europe to the Caribbean, Australia, and Fiji.

Bol and Brooks had the same desire to promote literacy and a love of reading, from Nebraska to Nigeria, but they were coming from a much different background than Carnegie. Bol had grown up with dyslexic leanings, so he had struggled with reading and hadn't always thought of books as friends. And the Little Free Library project certainly wasn't backed by Carnegie's millions: In fact, for the first few years, the Libraries were pieced together on the deck in Bol's backyard with nothing but elbow grease and upcycled materials. Add to that the fact that neither Bol nor Brooks were professional woodworkers ("What a competent carpenter can do in ten hours, I can do in forty or fifty—and not as well," Bol jokes), and it's a wonder that the project ever got off the ground.

But one by one, the handcrafted Little Libraries began to pop up across Wisconsin and Minnesota. Delighted neighbors traded books and told their friends. Soon, word of mouth, an NPR interview, and a few well-placed articles introduced them to other states across the country, and more were installed. Then more. In May of 2012, Little Free Library was established as an official nonprofit organization.

Soon after, that August, Little Free Library reached their goal of building 2,510 libraries to beat Carnegie's impressive number—a year and a half before their target date. And then, things exploded. By 2014, the number of Little Free Libraries had more than quadrupled, blowing Carnegie completely out of the water.

Today Little Free Libraries are a full-fledged—if still humbly grassroots—global movement. There are Libraries in Ukraine, Honduras, Iceland, and Pakistan; China, Italy, Ghana, and Japan; India, Australia, Netherlands, and Korea. They stand in big cities like New York and Los Angeles as well as in the smallest towns of Iowa and Idaho. They're planted in parks, cafés, and hospital waiting rooms, but mostly they are friendly beacons in our collective front yards.

Little Free Library stewards—the caretakers who build, install, stock, and tend to the Libraries—are what keep the movement inspired, say Bol and Brooks. Many of them have discovered ways to use their Libraries to accomplish amazing things, big and small. One woman in India is bringing a thousand Little Free Libraries to underserved students in her country. Inmates of a midwestern prison build the Libraries as a way to give back to society. Award-winning architects in Manhattan designed ten modern Little Free Libraries to bring a greater sense of community to the city streets. A college grad in North Carolina raised more than ten thousand dollars on Kickstarter for a single LFL. A five-year-old boy in Qatar worked with his dad to put up a Little Library in their new village to make it feel like home. Stewards in Minnesota turned their Little Free Libraries into makeshift seed exchanges to share flower, herb, and vegetable seeds with neighbors. And a man in a remote area of Georgia made his Little Library a geocaching site to attract visitors to his quiet country road.

Through the ingenuity of stewards like these, Little Free Libraries and the books they hold are being put into action in ways that Bol and Brooks had never imagined. "Little Free Libraries are turning regular people into heroes in their communities," Bol says.

And the Little Libraries—wildly diverse and inventive—are amazing in their own right. There are steward-built Libraries covered in bottle caps, whittled from tree trunks, made from old pinball machines, wearing hand-knit sweaters, or constructed to look like robots and Volkswagen buses, all a testament to the power of everyday creativity. Little Free Library itself offers more than a dozen models—like the Scandinavian Cottage, Red Sky Amish, Blue Tobacco Barn, and Urban Reader—which are for sale through their website for $175 and up. These are made by a handful of builders, including Bol and an Old Order Amish carpenter named Henry Miller who has constructed more than two thousand LFLs by hand.

All of this creative effort nudged Little Free Libraries further into the media spotlight, which in turn helped accelerate the Libraries' spread. *Reader's Digest* named Little Free Libraries one of their "50 Surprising Things We Love about America," right after sliced bread. "We beat Bruce Springsteen and Bon Jovi—and Bill Gates!" Bol says. "Who ever saw that coming?"

**The Original
Little Free Librarian**

The Little Free Library movement isn't the first time books have been shared in unconventional ways. As long as books have been around, they've been traded—whether hand to hand or through freecycle boxes at today's coffee shops and office break rooms.

Little Free Libraries were especially inspired by Lutie Stearns, a quirky and adventurous librarian who brought more than a thousand traveling libraries to every corner of Wisconsin between 1895 and 1914, when the public library system was still in its infancy.

Like a literary Johnny Appleseed, Stearns hauled boxes of books by train, coach, and sleigh to reach even the most remote settlements and set up temporary libraries in public spots like general stores and post offices.

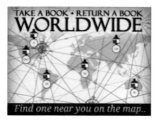

A Global Sensation

Where in the world is your local Little Free Library? A global map on the Little Free Library website aims to catalog every Library's exact location—down to latitude and longitude. Use the impressive map to find Little Free Libraries near you, track down Libraries when you're on the road, or locate the LFLs you'd love to visit someday. With a picture of each Little Library, GPS coordinates, a physical address, and often an e-mail address too, not only does the map show you where the Libraries sit, it connects you to the people who steward them. Find the map at littlefreelibrary.org/ourmap.

The *Huffington Post* has called Little Free Libraries "a global sensation." They've been featured on NBC *Nightly News*, CNN, NPR, and Japanese television and have appeared in the pages of *Parade, Better Homes and Gardens,* French and Italian fashion magazines, and hundreds of local papers. They've been the subject of multiple documentaries, including *Because It's Small* by Marc Kornblatt and *A Small Wooden Box* by Gwen Briesemeister (which can be seen on YouTube). Folk songs and children's songs have been written about them. In addition, the organization has received accolades from the National Book Foundation, which presented Little Free Library with an Innovations in Reading Prize, and the American Library Association, which gave them a Movers and Shakers Award.

But the founders don't take credit for the acclaim. "It's really about the people and the neighborhoods," Bol says. "We're representing them—the thousands of Little Free Library stewards and millions of supporters."

Brooks agrees. "I think we owe the success of this little social invention to the early adopters and first stewards who saw the possibilities and embraced the idea right away," he says. "They were enthusiastic and selfless about it, not in it for themselves or for profit, but for the sheer joy and simple generosity associated with every part of the mission. Buddhists have a name for that: altruistic joy. Just about every steward who has ever built or organized the establishment of a Little Library has done so for the greater good. They built it or bought it for the neighbors."

From the start, Little Free Library has stoked this altruistic spirit by using their Libraries to build stronger communities close to home and not so close to home. Today they keep up this mission through the Give It Forward Team (GIFT) Fund, a philanthropic piece of the organization that gathers donations to do good on small and large scales. The GIFT Fund provides grants to people who can't afford to buy a Little Free Library of their own. It also supports four programs:

- *Little Free Libraries for Small Towns,* which is working to bring LFLs to the eleven thousand towns in the United States without public libraries.
- *Books around the Block,* which partners with cities and schools to plant Little Free Libraries where kids and adults need better access to books.
- *Friends through the Years,* a partnership with the AARP Foundation to encourage intergenerational connections through books and to reduce feelings of isolation in older adults.
- *Good Global Neighbors,* which is getting books into the hands of readers everywhere. There are already Little Free Libraries in North America, South America, Asia, Africa, and Australia—from the streets of Milan to the refugee camps of Uganda. Next up: the team is working to bring a Little Library to Antarctica.

The engine that keeps this little, big idea moving is still fueled by one simple thing: the exchange of books between neighbors. And that pool of neighbors keeps getting bigger. Conservative estimates from Little Free Library say that in a single year, more than 35 million books are traded in the 25 thousand Little Libraries around the world, and for every book donated or taken, several people stop to peruse the selection. That means the Libraries are getting as many as 100 million visits per year.

Now, after serving as the place where so many books have changed hands, Little Free Libraries have a book of their own. Part idea book, part inspiration gallery, and part biography of the Little Free Library movement and its stewards, *The Little Free Library Book* is chockablock with stories to inspire.

First, read why we love these little boxes of books (or at least some thoughts on why we might). Then explore how Little Free Libraries are putting books into action—kickstarting community, literacy, creativity, and compassion across the country and the world. Each chapter profiles some of the most fascinating Little Free Libraries and citizen librarians around. Alongside are suggestions for using your Library to its fullest potential. You'll learn how to build and launch a Little Free Library as well as creative ways to engage your neighborhood, like orchestrating a Little Free Library block party, planning bike tours of local Little Free Libraries, organizing Library build days for communities in need, writing round robin–style stories with Library visitors, or curating a communal sketchbook. In addition, you'll find an appendix of practical advice, with construction plans, installation instructions, a clever way to yarn bomb your Library, and more.

So welcome! We're glad you're here. Look inside, flip through the chapters, mark your favorite pages, and find something that speaks to you. Just like in a Little Free Library, there are lots of stories and ideas to share.

A Library by Any Other Name

Before they were called "Little Free Libraries," cofounders Todd Bol and Rick Brooks had a running list of name ideas, including: House of Stories, Habitat for the Humanities, Box of Magic, and simply Free Book Exchange. The term Little Free Library is an homage to Andrew Carnegie's Carnegie Free Library system.

"A big question for us now is what to call them in places where English is not the primary language," says Brooks. "In Latin America, for instance, Biblioteca Libre, Bibliotequina, Casa de Libros, Case de Historias, and the generic Little Free Library are all still in the running. In French, Maison des Livres."

Why Little Free Libraries?

*"What is more important
in a library
than anything else—
than everything else—
is the fact that it exists."*

—ARCHIBALD MACLEISH

CHAPTER 1
WHY LITTLE FREE LIBRARIES?

It took three days and two trips to the hardware store to hunt down the perfect shade of yellow paint for our Little Free Library door.

Looking back, it's possible (o.k., *likely*) that I put too much thought into it, but I wanted the color to echo the spirit of the Little Library. It should be friendly but not shrill, welcoming but not overbearing, bright but not blazing—an arm waving our neighbors over, signaling that this was a place to stop, hang out, and connect. Turns out it was a tough checklist to satisfy: Lemon Meringue was too light. Marigold, too dark. Babouche, too subtle. Forsythia, Citrus, and Daisy, not right. Somewhere in the middle, though, was Sun Porch—even the name was inviting. I brushed on two coats.

When the paint dried and my husband and I planted the Little Free Library in front of our Harriet Avenue bungalow in Minneapolis, we weren't expecting magic to happen, with trumpets sounding and doves flying from the bushes. But within five minutes of getting it in the ground, something simple and significant took root. Our first visitors came: a mother and daughter from the house kitty-corner to ours, whom we rarely saw or spoke to. They crossed the wide street to check out the Library's fox-head handle and tobacco-lath trim, look through the inventory, and talk about summer T-ball leagues. It was the longest conversation we'd had in six years on the same block, and it was lovely. They also dropped off our first donation—a copy of the book *Little Miss Sunshine* by Roger Hargreaves, one that I remembered having on my childhood bookshelf.

This little box works, I thought.

The next morning, as I was heading to my car, a woman I'd never met struck up a conversation as she flipped through the Library to find a title she liked. Now, to be honest, pre–Little Free Library, I might have pretended to rummage in my bag to avoid an interaction with a stranger on the sidewalk. Or bent down to adjust my boot. Or anything, really. But the Library gave us a reason to connect. I found out that she was a public librarian who lived only a block away, and that she knew every Little Free Library in the neighborhood. We chatted about books, the sunrise, and potholes, and she said she'd come back often.

Our corner of the city seemed to get friendlier in other ways, too, as people not only stopped to visit the Library, but also to mention that a neighbor was ill, let us know that they would be gone on an extended trip, say hi to our kids, or to ask some small favor, like borrowing a ladder or ten minutes of our time to help with a project. We had trusted them to come into our yard and visit our new Little Library, smudging the line between private and public space. In turn, they trusted us back.

And over the following weeks and months, those neighbors brought book after book, ensuring that our Library—which had essentially become all of ours—remained full. They dropped off *This Is How You Lose Her* and *Lives of the Monster Dogs; The Brontës: Selected Poems, The Book Thief,* and *Billy Bathgate;* and wonderful oddballs like the biography of Chuck Norris and a book of verse called *There's an Awful Lot of Weirdos in Our Neighborhood.*

Through all the interactions and all the books, we kept the magic going, whatever it was. I suspect a can of Sun Porch yellow didn't have a thing to do with it.

Thousands of Little Free Libraries, like my modest example, stand in cities, small towns, and remote villages all over the world. Go to the map on Little Free Library's website, and you'll find a treasure map of the miniature Libraries—complete with GPS coordinates—from Juneau, Alaska, to Como, Italy, to Hanoi, Vietnam.

While researching this book, I found a common thread among all their stewards and supporters, even amid the diversity of cultural, educational, and economic backgrounds: an unstoppable enthusiasm for the Little Libraries, felt bone deep. Stewards everywhere were eager to tell stories about them, send photos, give design details, and share ideas, hoping they would inspire someone else to build one. Patrons said they planned road trips and bike rides, specifically to visit the Libraries. Even local realtors were enthusiastic—they said that if a Little Free Library is on the block, a house will sell faster.

But why all the love? What is it about these hand-built boxes of books that inspires us?

The excitement surrounding Little Free Libraries is something that cofounder Todd Bol is still trying to figure out. "It's like with puppies," he says. "Even when people are grouchy or growly, they see a puppy and say 'Oh, puppy!' in a high-pitched voice and a better, sweeter side of humanity comes jumping out. Now, when I talk to people about Little Free Libraries, they do the same thing: 'Oh, I love Little Free Libraries!' They'll pitch their voice and get all excited. It's almost a primal reaction—I think there's a primal desire to be connected and close to your community, and connected to each other. It's a reflection of a better spirit that's inside of us."

I asked the visitors to my Little Free Library if they had an answer, leaving a notebook and pen so they could explain why the Little Library movement is meaningful to them.

"It makes me feel like I'm a part of something good," wrote one visitor.

"It's just so human," wrote another.

Little Free Libraries bring us together.

The feeling of warmth and community is certainly one of the reasons Little Free Libraries move so many people. Our social connections are key to a full and rewarding life, whether we find them at a book club, an art opening, or a bridge game; a synagogue, a happy hour, or a PTA meeting; a community garden, a baseball field, or the Little Free Library down the street.

Through dozens of common spaces and events like these, we deepen our sense of belonging and build "social capital," the term Harvard University professor of public policy Robert Putnam uses to describe the value of our social networks (and not the ones you can find online). Social capital increases whenever we create new bonds, strengthen old ones, or work together for the greater good. An old-school barn raising on the prairie frontier is a classic example of social capital in action. But even something as small as adding a book to a Little Free Library, helping a motorist fix a flat tire, or nodding hello to a fellow jogger on a morning run can contribute to this collective investment.

And the payoff is big. According to research gathered at the Saguaro Seminar at Harvard, an initiative founded by Putnam, communities with higher levels of social capital provide much richer, more productive lives. They're likely to have higher educational achievements, more effective governments, faster economic growth, and lower crime rates. Plus, the people living there are typically happier, healthier, and live longer. In fact, the Saguaro Seminar finds, joining and participating in a single new group cuts your odds of dying over the next year by half. (I'm not saying that starting a Little Free Library will save your life—but it couldn't hurt.)

Over the last two generations, though, there's been a shift in how we spend our time, and our social capital and connections to other people have suffered. We look at Facebook instead of visiting with friends face-to-face, and we binge-watch Netflix on our couches instead of hanging out at the movie theater. As our culture of work becomes increasingly pervasive and demanding, we're also inclined to stay plugged in to our jobs instead of plugging in to our families and neighbors.

Little Free Libraries are a small but potent antidote to this erosion of connectedness. Their doors are always open, and the invitation to visit is a standing one. The benefits of a Little Library can come from the anodyne interactions on the sidewalk that help build friendships and trust, as well as from larger community-building efforts. A neighborhood that gets together for a grand opening party at a new Little Free Library, for example, feels the positive effects of good company and strengthened community ties. A group that meets to build Little Libraries for places where books are scarce gets to know each other and feels a larger, human connection to other parts of the world.

By its nature, a Little Free Library is a kind of collectivizer. It gathers people to create it, to participate in it, and to share in it, and it reminds us that we can be better together.

Little Free Libraries are people sized.

One scholar attributes the success of Little Free Libraries to two things: they're achievable, and they're self-sustaining.

"I think an awful lot of things that spread at the local level are people sized. Doable," says John McKnight, codirector of the Asset-Based Community Development Institute at Northwestern University and author of the book *The Abundant Community.* "Little Free Library isn't daunting. And it isn't powered by money or gasoline or contributions—it's powered by books. I think most people have books that they've read and are willing to share with others or give away. So the fuel that runs the effort is free; it doesn't require lots of outside resources."

That means that Little Free Libraries are for everyone. Unlike larger projects, like planning a new city park or community center, building a Little Free Library is, as McKnight points out, gratifyingly doable. You don't have to be a professional contractor, you don't have to clear a lot of red tape, and you don't

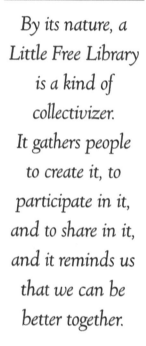

By its nature, a Little Free Library is a kind of collectivizer. It gathers people to create it, to participate in it, and to share in it, and it reminds us that we can be better together.

need a lot of money. The workload is reasonable: If you can't complete it in one weekend, you can be pretty confident that it will be done in three or four. And the materials are attainable—exotic woods and expensive trim aren't necessary; instead, many stewards find inventive ways to use recycled items.

Artist Suzanne Janse-Vreeling of Minneapolis only had to look as far as her workroom for building materials. "I made my Little Free Library out of leftover metal scraps in my studio," she says. "And the side panels are old tin ceiling pieces salvaged out of the garbage." Lisette Trombley of Renton, Washington, turned a kitchen appliance on the fritz into a Little Library. "I'm not much of a carpenter, so I was looking around for something inexpensive that was the right size and shape, as well as being weatherproof," she says. "Then, my microwave oven died. It occurred to me that it would be perfect as a Little Free Library." Other stewards have built their Libraries from wooden cabinets or unused suitcases, and yet others have found clever ways to raise money to purchase a Little Free Library from the organization, if the price tag is out of their reach.

Once the Library is up and running, it's largely a self-sustaining system. Although dedicated stewards are vital to tending the structure and curating the books inside, they shouldn't need to worry about running out of inventory. The "Take a Book, Return a Book" motto ensures that the shelves of books in a Little Free Library are in perpetual motion, thanks to the help of the generous patrons who visit.

Because the necessary resources—time, materials, and commitment—don't prohibit anyone from participating, and because a Little Library's door is open to everyone, the Little Free Library phenomenon feels wonderfully inclusive. If it's a people-sized movement, it's one size fits all, in the best possible way.

Little Free Libraries are vehicles for self-expression.

There are no rules when it comes to what Little Free Libraries look like. The majority are around two feet by two feet square and resemble a miniature house with a gently pitched roof. But this basic form is only a suggestion. Many Little Free Library designers, artists, and architects—both trained and self-taught—deviate from it to create inspired, unique Libraries.

There are Little Free Libraries that look like phone booths, fire stations, and fairy houses. They are beautifully tiled, collaged, and carved. Some are kinetic sculptures with moving parts. Others are painted to pay tribute to traditional Native American totems, Van Gogh masterpieces, art nouveau prints, or Dr. Seuss drawings.

Though the diversity of Libraries prohibits us from labeling the entire Little Free Library oeuvre an art movement, many of the Little Libraries—in their own way—are undeniable works of informal public art. Some can be classified as folk art, outsider art, or social practice art; and others are simple handcraft. But none have signs that say "Do Not Touch." They welcome interaction and exploration.

"Aesthetics are different for everybody—what people respond to—which is why I think that public art is good when it's diverse," says Kelly Pajek, cochair of the journal *Public Art Dialogue*. "Little Free Libraries tie, in the best circumstances, to public art. There's an element of surprise. It's something that you can publicly engage with—you're not being told that it's hands off, or that you can't participate—you're encouraged to be part of it. I think both of those things are certainly tenets of public art."

With so much freedom to hotrod your Little Free Library however you want, they also stand as a reflection of the maker. Maybe you want bright chevron stripes to echo your bright personality, or a buttoned-up, meticulously crafted Library to mirror the pride you take in your house. Maybe you want a seashell-covered Library to call out your affinity for the ocean or an urban skyline to celebrate your city. It's street art by your sidewalk, and it says a lot about you.

Because Little Free Libraries are often installed in walkable areas humming with pedestrian traffic, many people can view them many times a day. If every Library isn't a polished work of art, they can still offer an unexpected moment, bring joy, establish a sense of place, and make an impact—reminding the viewer that creativity is accessible, even in an otherwise familiar landscape.

And, of course, there're the books.

It's impossible to talk about the appeal of Little Free Libraries without talking about the hundreds of books that can cycle through them every day. This is why we truly love them. With no library card, no late fees, and no closing time, Little Free Libraries put books in our paths in a freewheeling way and are full of possibility.

A kid walking home from a bus stop might open a Little Library door and find a graphic novel that gets him excited about reading for the first time. A man on his way to work might discover a volume of poetry that changes his life. A girl out walking the family dog might pick up a landscape photography book that shows corners of the world she hopes to visit one day.

For many people, it's this sense of discovery that drives their devotion to Little Free Libraries. You never know what you'll find. Open that friendly door, and you could be introduced to an author who inspires you or a book that you never would have found on your own. Each title—whether a field guide to birds, a Lebanese cookbook, or a political biography—is a potential source of inspiration. And the infusion of new material is constant. Pass by a Little Free Library on your evening stroll, and the stock may be completely different from what was there in the morning.

A kind of literary voyeurism adds to this feeling of discovery. By peeking into the reading lives of the Little Free Library owner and other users in the neighborhood, you get to know the block better. Who put the 1,184-page copy of Haruki Murakami's *1Q84* in the Library? Was it so long that they gave up, or did they love it enough to share? Here is a copy of Harry Frankfurt's *On Bullshit*. Does a philosopher live nearby, or did someone just like the book's title? Who contributed all the yoga manuals and South American travel guides, and who left the hard-boiled detective novels? And where will my copy of *Pride and Prejudice* end up when I leave it in the Library to be discovered by someone else?

For Little Free Library stewards, sharing books is a meaningful element of the movement, in part because of this opportunity to be known. "I almost think of it as offering yourself on a platter," says Bol. "'Here are my books, here I am in the community, this is what's important to me. Books are a reflection of what I am, and I love them, and if I can share them with my neighbors, I'm sharing who I am.'"

NANCY PEARL

Librarian Nancy Pearl is so well known in library circles that she has her own action figure (with amazing push-button shushing action!). She's the author of *Book Lust: Recommended Reading for Every Mood, Moment, and Reason* and founded the pioneering "If All Seattle Read the Same Book" project, which has since been adopted by many other cities. Here, Pearl talks about her affection for Little Free Libraries, with some of her favorites included on pages 21–23 with other Seattle Little Free Libraries.

> "The thing I like about books, in general, is that they connect people, one to another, through a shared reading—whether they know that connection exists or not."
>
> —NANCY PEARL

Seattle is a hotbed for Little Free Libraries. Tell me about the Little Free Libraries in your neighborhood and when you like to visit them.

I do a daily walk of about seven miles, and on my daily walk, there are five Little Free Libraries. I deliberately plan my walk so I can visit each of them at least a couple times a week to see what's new.

It's just always so much fun. First of all, it's fun to happen upon one that you haven't known about before. But it's really fun to check to see what books are there, and to imagine (because of the books) what kind of person lives in that house.

For example, one of the houses that I go by has had a bunch of books related to the Vietnam War. One of them was *A Bright Shining Lie*, which is a wonderful nonfiction book about Vietnam, and I thought, "Well, that's interesting." Then a few days later, I was walking by and there was another book about the Vietnam War, which had been given to the donator by a veterans' group. So I jumped to conclusions and thought that surely someone living there was a Vietnam vet.

The thing I like about books, in general, is that they connect people, one to another, through a shared reading—whether they know that connection exists or not. So I'm always interested in the people who are reading the book.

What book would you be overjoyed to find in one of the Little Free Libraries you visit?

It's an older title called *Take Care of My Little Girl* by a woman named Peggy Goodin. I've never found it in a used bookstore, libraries don't have it anymore, and it's quite expensive online—or more expensive than I'm willing to pay—and I just want to read it again. That, I would be overjoyed to find in a Little Free Library.

MARGRET ALDRICH

I'm at the stage in my personal library where most of the books that I want, I have—even most of the older ones I've been able to collect. But *Take Care of My Little Girl* I have not. It's the story of a young girl who goes off to college and has to decide whether or not to join a sorority. On my daily walk, I go through the campus at the university every day on Fraternity Row, and I see all these fraternity and sorority houses, so if I haven't been thinking about *Take Care of My Little Girl* before the walk, it brings it back into my head.

Wouldn't it be something if you found it in a Little Free Library!
I guess that's the most fun thing about Little Free Libraries—the serendipity of them. What you're going to find and what somebody wants to share. I think that's great.

Do you think that's part of why they've become so popular?
I know from my library experience, the best way to get books to circulate is to put them on a book cart in the library and have a sign that says, "Your neighbor just returned this," or "Your neighbor just read this." Something that shows that these books have just been returned *by your neighbors.* Then people always go over there and go through the books.

Even though with Little Free Libraries and with those book carts, you don't know if your neighbor liked it or not, just the fact that somebody read it whom you know or whom you have something in common with or whom you live in the same neighborhood with leads people to pick up those books.

So I think it's that. I think at this point, too, what's fun about it is not only the books, but coming upon the books. Coming upon the Little Free Libraries themselves. Because they're not on every street, and finding one is like a little treat.

In Seattle, on one of the streets I walk down, we have a Little Free Library with "a poem a day," where this person puts in his box not books but poems that you can take every day. I also like in Seattle that people haven't built the Little Free Library kit; they've built their own. During the football season, one had a Seahawks head on it.

People who have Little Free Libraries love "real" libraries, too. Are conventional libraries and librarians generally supportive of the LFL movement?
I don't have a great imagination, but it's hard for me to imagine that anyone who loves to read doesn't just love those Little Free Libraries. It's a great good for society to have them.

IN GOOD COMPANY

A Little Free Library is only one example of sharing among strangers. Here are some other unconventional ways that we've traded, shared, and given away items—from books to bolt cutters.

Tool-lending libraries

One of the first official tool-lending programs started in Berkeley, California's public library system in 1979. Check out a ladder, weed eater, or cement mixer the same way you would check out a book.

Seed libraries

Exchange heirloom tomato, black-eyed Susan, and basil seeds at a local seed library. Often located in public libraries and community centers (and even Little Free Libraries), patrons can take seeds or share seeds to keep their gardens growing and encourage local biodiversity. The Seed Library Social Network (seedlibraries.org) has members from all over the world.

BookCrossing

Called "a modern-day message in a bottle" by the *San Francisco Chronicle,* the popular BookCrossing (bookcrossing.com) program is an interactive way to share books. Print a label with a special ID for your book, leave it for someone else to find—perhaps on a park bench, a coffee shop counter, or a Little Free Library shelf—then track it to see where it ends up.

The Uni Project

Don't have a place to sit and read in your neighborhood? The Uni Project (theuniproject.org) shares pop-up, open-air reading rooms—complete with bookshelves, books, and benches—where they're needed. The nonprofit group currently serves the New York area but can ship a reading room kit anywhere.

Free stores

In this kind of shop, everything is 100 percent off. Free stores—also known as swap shops—allow users to give or get items like furniture, books, and clothing at no cost. Book Thing, a brick-and-mortar free store in Baltimore, stocks nothing but books. (The catch? You can only take 150,000 free books per day.) The Freecycle Network (freecycle.org) operates like an online free store, with nearly eight million members worldwide.

Food swaps

Too many jars of homemade kimchi in your pantry? Trade them for some hand-foraged mushrooms or a dozen backyard eggs at a local food swap. The Food Swap Network (foodswapnetwork.com) helps home cooks, canners, bakers, brewers, and urban farmers barter their wares, reduce food waste, and make connections.

Free lodging

Who needs a hotel? Couchsurfing (couchsurfing.org) helps you find free accommodations. The tool connects you with locals in more than 120,000 cities around the world who are willing to let you sleep on their sofa or spare bed.

Get Started

LAUNCHING A LITTLE FREE LIBRARY

"The only thing that you absolutely have to know, is the location of the library."

—ALBERT EINSTEIN

CHAPTER 2
GET STARTED

There are more than twenty-five thousand Little Free Libraries around the world, and each has a one-of-a-kind origin story. Some were built by two hands, while others were built by ten. Some were constructed by master craftsmen, others by brave-hearted novices. They've been created to foster literacy, bring communities together, or satisfy an artistic itch, and they've been made to simply swap a few good books. But all Little Free Libraries have one thing in common: they each got started, thanks to the dedicated steward who brought them to life.

The relative ease of establishing one of these small book exchanges is part of the reason for the movement's success. Unlike larger humanitarian projects that can require months to complete, a Little Free Library is wonderfully doable—even for individuals working on their own. The start-up costs are low. It can be finished in a weekend or two. It's satisfyingly tangible. And the effects are immediately apparent, from the moment a visitor opens the Little Library door and chooses a book or shares one.

This chapter tells the first-step stories of an eclectic group of Little Free Libraries (starting with the very first one in existence) and explains how you can launch one of your own.

TODD BOL

Hudson, Wisconsin, USA

Charter Number: 1

The best ideas can come to us at the most unexpected times, swimming to the surface unbidden but welcome. For Todd Bol, the first Little Free Library was one of those charmed ideas, triggered by a lost job, a cross-country road trip, and a garage sale.

Bol has an unflappable entrepreneurial spirit and an idea generator that runs on overdrive: for every three good ideas he has, he's leaving thirty on the table. But when he was laid off in 2009 from the company he started with Global Scholarship Alliance, he was in his midfifties and not sure what to do next. "I was devastated when they closed down the Wisconsin office, which I thought was my life's dream and the accumulation of everything for me careerwise," he says.

Bol's wife, Susan, suggested that he go away for a while to clear his head, so he packed his bags and traveled around the country for a month. "It was a good, soul-searching thing to do," he says, "kind of a modern-day version of *Easy Rider*—except in a minivan."

After he returned home, Bol got to work turning his garage into an office, putting in windows and removing a vintage 1920s garage door. He had a talent for finding new uses for old objects and thought the wood was too nice to get rid of—he wanted to do something respectful with it. After staring at the door for a few months, Bol decided to build a model one-room schoolhouse in honor of his mother, June Bol, a former teacher and a lifelong reader. As he thought about his mom during the construction process, he said to himself, "Maybe we'll put books in it."

Then on a Saturday in May 2010 came the garage sale that launched a thousand Libraries: the Bols hosted a sale in their front yard, and Todd mounted the schoolhouse full of hardcovers and paperbacks on a post. It was the first Little Free Library, though it wasn't called that yet. As the day went on, neighbor after neighbor was drawn to the Library, stopping to admire it, ask about it, buzz around it, browse through it, and generally get excited about it.

"When I saw how people responded to the Little Free Library, my next question was: Would more people respond to it? Is this just a fluke of nature? Is it something in the air? Is it springtime?" Todd wondered. "As with most ideas, when you think you've got a decent one, what you have to say to yourself is, 'How do I test this out?'"

MARGRET ALDRICH

An older neighbor who liked the schoolhouse Library tipped Bol off to an old barn that had been knocked over by a tornado—the barn wood would be good material for more Libraries. Bol built another half dozen. Library Number Two started out in a friend's garden, then traveled to a gallery called Absolutely Art in Madison, Wisconsin, with the help of Rick Brooks, whom Bol had gotten to know after hearing him speak on community sustainability practices. They staked a few more Libraries in Madison, but by that winter had sold only one. After another sale or two, they decided to start planting seeds by giving them away. Then Brooks's son encouraged them to apply for a grant from the Chicago Awesome Foundation. Through that program, they were awarded one thousand dollars to establish six more Libraries and were featured on Illinois public radio. The real boosts came from an article published in *Wisconsin Journal* and a guest appearance on Jean Feraca's Wisconsin public radio show *Here on Earth*.

"At that point, we were struggling," Bol says. "But the day after the show, when I was driving to see our Amish carpenter, Henry, and I stopped on the side of the road to read my map, a guy knocked on my window. I thought, Uh-oh, what'd I do, but when I rolled down the window, he said 'Jean Feraca?' I said, 'No, I'm Todd Bol.' And he said, 'No, no, no—I heard you on Jean Feraca.' I had a Little Free Library loaded on my trailer, so I was easy to identify. Then I stopped at the bank, and an eighty-year-old man waved at me and said, 'Jean Feraca!'" Within another month or two, Little Free Libraries were featured in *USA Today* and then on NBC *Nightly News*.

Soon after, Bol and Brooks started getting more and more requests from all over the world from people who wanted a Little Library of their own, and they established Little Free Library as a nonprofit organization. But the project remained—and still is—a grassroots effort in the spirit of the original Little Library. "The funny part is," Todd says, "up until November 2012, I was building Libraries on my deck and staining them in my shed where my freezer is, in a teeny six-by-six space. I got a kick out of sending Libraries and signs to different countries knowing that I was doing it with a twenty-dollar garage sale saw on my back deck in Wisconsin." (Now the organization has office and workspace in Hudson. It's home to a sturdy wooden conference table hand-built by Bol, Little Free Libraries in various stages of construction, and an entire room devoted to decorative embellishments.)

Bol began getting letters and e-mails thanking him for starting Little Free Library. One fan told him that, at Halloween, the kids on her street were more excited by her Library than they were about candy. Another steward told him, "Little Free Libraries are better than the moon."

Though he recognizes the impact that Little Free Libraries have, Bol gives all the credit to the stewards who start up Libraries in their neighborhoods. And rather than the Wizard of Oz, he compares himself to Dorothy—all he did, he says, was stumble on the Tin Man and apply a shot of oil to get him moving. "I know this is an established thing that has touched many people's hearts, and the world is a better place for it, but it's because of the people in the communities," Bol says. "I was just fortunate to be able to show them an option."

He encourages new stewards to keep the movement going and advocates building from recycled materials, being creative with what you have, connecting with people, and having a good time in the process. "It's the easiest thing in the world to get started," he says. "If you don't have the money to buy one from us, start talking to your neighbors. I know a woman in Hawaii who walked down to her local Home Depot and explained what a Little Free Library was, and they built one for her. And another neighbor brought it from Home Depot to her house, and another man put it up for her. It's a natural thing to bring communities together."

The first Little Free Library—that red schoolhouse in Bol's front yard—is still there, and it still gets regular visitors. Now it has a partner: a Library built in honor of his dad made from family relics like his great-grandma's quilting rack, a piece of an old sleigh, and a music box that his mother gave his father more than fifty years ago, cleverly rigged to play "The Impossible Dream" every time someone opens the Library's door. When the time comes, the Wisconsin Historical Society hopes to preserve his mom's schoolhouse Library in their archive.

"When my mom died, I gave everyone at the funeral a necklace that said, 'June A. Bol, a dancing spirit, 1927–' and the premise was an old saying that you never die until all that you've touched has passed away," Bol says. "What's really cool is that my mom inspired this, and now she's dancing all over the place, inspiring people all around the world."

> *"Little Free Libraries are better than the moon."*
>
> —ANONYMOUS
> LITTLE FREE LIBRARY FAN

MARGRET ALDRICH

SWAPNA KRISHNA

Washington, DC, USA

Charter Number: 10164

Putting up a new Little Free Library can keep overly anxious stewards up at night: What if no one uses it? What if too many people use it? And what if it's impossible to keep stocked? Book blogger Swapna Krishna finds that she has nothing to worry about in this essay, which first appeared on bookriot.com, when a symbiotic relationship between her Little Free Library and her DC neighbors naturally falls into place.

"When we bought a house in late 2012 in the urban neighborhood of Capitol Hill, DC, those little boxes of book love called Little Free Libraries were just starting to make the news. Of course I'd heard of them, and considering we live on a busy street with lots of foot traffic across from a huge park, I longed to put one in our front yard. Capitol Hill is a literary neighborhood, and I was sure all my neighbors would partake (plus it'd give me something to do with the overabundance of books I receive from my blog, *S. Krishna's Books*).

I tested my theory out over the course of a few weekends, putting boxes of books out for the taking. And oh man, they went like hotcakes—sometimes ten books in an hour. I started to get a little nervous. I still wanted to do the Little Free Library, but would I be able to keep it filled? Would it sit there like a shell of a Library, feeling unwanted and abandoned because I didn't have enough books to slake my neighbors' thirst for reading material? (Yes, I got a little dramatic. I'm an anxious person. It happens.)

Fast-forward a year to January 2014. My husband's parents arrived for a post-Christmas visit . . . with a little surprise in tow. My mother-in-law heard me mentioning my desire for a Little Free Library over Thanksgiving, and what did they do? *They built me one. From scratch.* Using wood and tools and screws and all sorts of things. And then, just to be awesome (and with my husband's guidance), they painted it to match my house.

Possibly the most fun part of having the Little Free Library was watching people discover it. (Yes, I've been spying on all of you. We have big bay windows in front of our house, so yes, I sit on my couch with my books and spy.) People would cut across the street from the park then see this structure in front of the house. So many people actually turned around, going out of their way to explore. I let our local listserv know about it, and I got so many e-mails from my neighbors thanking me, telling me it fit in so well with the character of our neighborhood.

Those first couple of weeks were a whirlwind. Over the course of six days, I had twenty-two books checked out. *Twenty-two. In six days.* So of course, I started to really panic. How was I going to keep things full?

But then something happened. Something awesome that completely reinforces how much I love my neighborhood. Books started showing up. Not returned, but new books (or at least, new to the Library) started appearing. And I'm not talking about old, yellowed textbooks or well-worn mass-market paperbacks (though, yes, there have been quite a few of those). I'm talking Dave Eggers, Barbara Kingsolver, Alexander McCall Smith, Haruki Murakami, Cassandra Clare, and Kathryn Stockett, just to name a few.

More and more books arrive every day; it's gotten to the point where my neighbors have taken it upon themselves to fill up the Library as it gets emptied (or more likely, they, too, are delighted with this new outlet for them to get rid of their old books, but I prefer the more noble interpretation). I still curate (most of those old yellowed books don't survive my cullings), switching out books and adding more as necessary, but the thing has taken on a life of its own to be sure.

Putting in the Little Free Library (or really, watching my father-in-law and husband dig into the semifrozen ground on a twenty-degree day in January from the comfort of a warm house) was one of the best things I've done since moving to my new house. Every day, it's a delight to go out and see what's shown up and what's been taken, to make deductions and suppositions on my neighbors' reading tastes based on what disappears immediately and what lingers.

My Little Free Library has already become an institution in my neighborhood, with regular visitors, and I can't wait to see where it goes from here. 🙶

MARGRET ALDRICH

HOW TO START A LITTLE FREE LIBRARY

Here is the rundown of what you need to know to start your very own Little Free Library, from choosing the perfect spot to filling it with books. You can do it! The only things you need are the desire to share a love of reading, commitment to taking care of your Library, and passion for making your block a better place.

Pick a location

Many stewards choose to plant their Little Free Library in their front yard, close to a sidewalk and the footfalls of pedestrian traffic. But others have found public places that could benefit from a Library, such as parks, school-yards, hospital waiting rooms, and apartment lobbies. If your Library will venture outside your property, be sure to get the location approved before breaking ground.

Get your Library

There are several ways to go about getting a Little Free Library:

1) You can order one that's already built from littlefreelibrary.org. There are more than a dozen different styles to choose from, including the Amish Barn Wood Cabin, the Urban Reader, the Little Red British Phone Booth Library, and the Blue Tobacco Barn. Some models are completely finished, while others are ready for you to paint.

2) You can order a kit from littlefreelibrary.org to put together yourself. With this option, you get the satisfaction of hammering some nails without the pressure of using a circular saw. (And, let's be honest, some of us book lovers should not be around a power tool that could take off a finger.)

3) You can build one yourself. A Little Free Library can look however you want it to look—there are no requirements or limits. Go ahead and build a replica of your house or a tiny Taj Mahal. Use an old mailbox or bathroom

cabinet for materials. Or follow the suggested plans on page 225 or on the Little Free Library website.

Make it official

A Little Free Library isn't a true-blue Little Free Library until you register it at littlefreelibrary.org. Once you've registered, the organization will send you a hand-finished sign with your official charter number, to attach to your Library; an informational packet that includes outreach tools, a bumper sticker, and bookplates; details on opportunities to get free books; and a list of ways to connect with other stewards. Now you're part of a global club of people devoted to growing community and literacy around the world.

Install your Library

To get your Little Free Library in the ground, follow the mounting instructions on page 243 or on the Little Free Library website. Be sure to check for gas lines, cables, or tree roots before you dig. If you want to keep the Library under wraps until a grand opening, cover it with a sheet or garbage bag tied with a bow. (That'll get the neighbors' attention.)

Stock your Library

Fill your Library with books you're excited to share. Glean from your own collection or visit used bookstores and thrift shops to buy affordable inventory. You can also contact local libraries and bookstores to find out if they're willing to donate good-quality books that are ready to be taken out of circulation. Just be sure to leave some room so neighbors can drop off books, too!

Get the word out

Your beautiful new Little Free Library is finished. Now's the time to tell everyone you know that it's open for business—and to celebrate. See "Launching Your Library" on page 54 for ideas.

Put it on the map

Add your Little Free Library's location and photos to the official world map at littlefreelibrary.org. The map is an impressive resource for discovering where Little Libraries can be found, near and far.

KYLE, GINNY, AND FINN PENNEKAMP

Los Angeles, California, USA

Charter Number: 1925

A combination of book love and sleep deprivation inspired screenwriter Kyle Pennekamp and former movie producer Ginny Pennekamp to install their Little Free Library. "We were deep into a period of absolutely no sleep with our six-month-old son. We felt we needed something to reconnect us to people in the outside world—the world where people didn't have to choose between reading and sleeping—and to the books that we loved so much," they say.

They were also spurred by a newfound drive to make the world a friendlier, more connected place for young Finn. "Once we had a kid, we discovered a desire in ourselves that pre-responsibility-for-another-human-life Kyle and Ginny never could have imagined: the desire to be generous and put down roots in a community. To spread the kind of love that you hope will come back to your child in the future. The love of reading."

The Library itself is decorated to celebrate books. The sides of the Library are painted with the Pennekamp's favorite words and ideas from books: Oz,

Create, Write, Call Me Ishmael, Expecto Patronum, 007, Huck Finn (for their son Finn), and The Artful Dodger (for their dog Dodger). It also features miniature versions of their favorite titles—*Carter Beats the Devil*, *Lonesome Dove*, *Time Regained*, *Moby-Dick*, and others—hanging from the trim.

"They're the books that are most meaningful in our lives. We read all of Proust in a year-and-a-half-long book group at Skylight Books. There were six of us left in the end. It was a truly profound experience for all of us," they say. "We read *Moby-Dick* together by listening to the Moby-Dick Big Read (moby-dickbigread.com) while we fed a one-year-old Finn. He's probably the only one-year-old that's ever 'read' the entirety of *Moby-Dick*."

Though their first attempt at building a Little Free Library wasn't exactly successful—the hinges were on the wrong side of the door, the roof rusted, and the whole Library fell off the fence a few times (let's chalk that up to sleep deprivation, too)—it's become a popular destination in the neighborhood that draws families and more unusual visitors. One couple, who had traveled to California from South Africa, made sure to stop by the Pennekamp's Library after seeing it featured on Airbnb's Los Feliz homepage. Another group came from a nearby television shoot.

"One week, a bunch of doctors in scrubs kept coming to the Library, and both Kyle and I noticed them hanging around and looking at the books," Ginny says. "We were out in the yard early one Friday night, and two doctors came by. They said everyone from their work knew about it, and they were walking there on their break. We said, 'Hey! Awesome! We'll stock some more science books and stuff doctors like.' They said, 'Oh. We're not doctors. We're actors. We just play doctors on *Grey's Anatomy*.'"

The Pennekamps' Little Free Library is thriving on Russell Avenue and is even the subject of a short documentary, directed by Sam Friedman (view it here: vimeo.com/68884904). At this point, it's hard to imagine the neighborhood without it.

"We used to add books to the Library every now and then, and we still keep a stack of books in the house for that purpose, but after the first full year of existence, we're happy to report that the Little Free Library #1925 was and remains about 98 percent self-sustaining," the Pennekamps say. "It's not ours anymore. It's Los Feliz's."

SARAH MAXEY

Winston-Salem, North Carolina, USA

Charter Number: Multiple

With lumber to buy, hardware to purchase, and books to collect, starting up a Little Free Library can feel like a big challenge—especially when you don't have a lot of resources. That's why recent college graduate Sarah Maxey got creative. She used the crowdfunding website Kickstarter to raise money—as well as worldwide support—for a Little Library in Winston-Salem, North Carolina. In the process, she launched her project into LFL history.

"In July of 2013, I was browsing Kickstarter, and a Little Free Library campaign in Portland was featured on the homepage. The project's image—the iconic wooden box with books—caught my eye and sparked curiosity in me," Maxey says. Since moving back to her hometown after college, she had been looking for ways to reconnect with her community, and stewarding a small, shared library seemed like a perfect way to do that.

But before she could get the project started, Maxey needed to rally the funding to build and stock a Library. "From my research, it seemed that Little Free Libraries thrive when people feel some ownership of them, so I also decided to host a Kickstarter campaign," she says. Incentives for funders included hand-printed bookmarks, books dedicated in the donor's name, or, for those who donated more than fifty dollars, their name inscribed on the Little Free Library itself.

When Maxey shared the project on her personal Facebook page, she expected a handful of close friends and family to donate pocket change to the cause, but within a few hours, she had reached her $175 goal.

The real shock came a few days later, when donations suddenly skyrocketed. "At the beginning of my volunteer shift at the local hospital, I had raised around $300," Maxey says. "When I checked my phone on the way out of the hospital, a mere three hours later, I had over $2,000 in funding: my project had been featured on the Kickstarter newsletter, which is sent to thousands of subscribers worldwide!"

The next few weeks were a whirlwind for Maxey, as her Kickstarter funding total continued to climb, and people from all over the world sent her messages of encouragement. By the end of the thirty-day campaign, 586 people had donated an astounding $10,402 to her personal Little Free Library project—more than any individual had ever raised for a single LFL. "It was clear that I would no longer be building one Little Free Library, but that I would be building dozens of Libraries locally, and perhaps even nationally," she says.

With more than ten thousand dollars earmarked for Little Free Libraries, Maxey began collecting books and getting to know her hometown once again. "I've already connected with so many great people that I would have never had contact with had it not been for the Little Free Library project," she says.

And Winston-Salem didn't leave Maxey to build all those Little Free Libraries alone. That fall, she worked with Kelly Mitter, the local director of the Neighborhood Revitalization Program of Habitat for Humanity, to plan a community build at their facility. "Around twenty volunteers, many of whom had no previous construction experience, gathered on a chilly November Saturday and built thirteen Little Free Libraries in just four hours," Maxey says.

One of Maxey's favorite parts of the project has been coming home to book donations—lots of book donations—on her front porch. "Just last week, I received a shipment from a man who had carefully selected fourteen books from his collection and placed quotes on the inside flaps that embodied the message of each book," she says. "One of my favorites from that donation was Mitch Albom's *Tuesdays with Morrie,* accompanied by the quote, 'No act of kindness, no matter how small, is ever wasted.'"

For Maxey, what started out as a small idea to launch one Little Free Library turned into an ongoing project, larger than she had ever anticipated. And she's not going to waste a day of it. "I plan to continue creating Libraries, finding happy stewards, and stocking the structures with books until the funds run out," she says.

UMAYR ANSARI

Al Wakrah, Qatar

Charter Number: 4621

The first Little Free Library in the Middle East was launched by a young boy and his father in Qatar. Umayr's Little Library is stocked with the kind of books that every young reader can appreciate, like *A Hatful of Seuss*, *Guinness Book of World Records*, *Bob's Busy Screwdriver*, *The Farm Book*, *D. W. Rides Again*, and *Ripley's Believe It or Not!* The letter he wrote (with the help of his dad) tells its story.

"My name is Umayr. I am five years old and live in Qatar with my dad Khalid, mom Yasmin, and older brother Saad. Our Little Free Library is named after me: Umayr's Little Free Library (or ULFL). We moved from Canada to Qatar three years back.

When my dad first moved to Qatar (with us still back in Canada), he got a sense that there were not very many accessible public libraries there. Since we all love to read, he asked us to pack all the books and get them here. We had several boxes just of books!

We live in a company compound with sixty villas in Al Wakrah, which is a small town just outside Doha (the capital and only big city in Qatar). As we settled in and made friends, I started sharing my books with them. People would regularly visit to borrow books from me. While we started lending out books, we thought of how we could do this efficiently. We thought of starting a mini library with the usual check-in, check-out system. During this time my mom, Yasmin, started looking online for how to go about starting a private library, and stumbled upon the Little Free Library. This was exactly what we wanted.

It took us awhile to get the library box made locally here with the help of a carpenter. We then painted it at home. The compound maintenance people gladly built us a small pedestal outside our house for the box.

Once we opened the Little Free Library, it was an instant hit. Lots of kids from the compound and some adults thronged to it. My mom and dad started a Facebook page for the little library (facebook.com/UmayrsLittleFreeLibrary), which recently got more than a hundred "likes." Umayr's LFL was also covered by local online news outlet, *Doha News,* and got encouraging comments.

The library is doing quite good. At evening time you can see kids from the compound gather around the ULFL. We are hoping this idea will catch on and some Little Free Libraries will spring up in other parts of Qatar as well. Some people have contacted us via our Facebook page on how to go about it, and several people have donated books. We're really glad to have this going. I am always excited about it. It's something I look forward to checking every day when I return from school. **"**

PEN WORLD VOICES FESTIVAL
AND THE ARCHITECTURAL LEAGUE OF NEW YORK

New York, New York, USA

Charter Number: Multiple

New York is home to many of the world's most recognizable architectural icons—the Statue of Liberty, the Empire State Building, St. Patrick's Cathedral, the Guggenheim—and now it's home to some remarkable Little Free Libraries as well. In May 2013, the PEN World Voices Festival and the Architectural League of New York enlisted local architects to design ten Little Libraries fit for the city.

"We were interested to see how New York city design firms would reenvision the Little Free Library concept," says Anne Rieselbach, program director at the Architectural League of New York. The results were wonderfully eclectic, with Libraries that resembled fishbowls, UFOs, trellises, and mirrored boxes.

"Some architects created site-specific pieces; others created more freestanding structures that would be easily replicable on any site," Rieselbach says. "What is so interesting is how many of the New York City architects chose an approach that in many cases created a place to sit and read or talk—either through incorporating existing infrastructure like park benches, building their own integral seating, or through other design features. Nevertheless, they all shelter books—the same basic 'program' as the prototypical Little Free Libraries."

The Libraries were placed in public spaces all over Lower Manhattan, stocked with books donated by publishers, and tended by community organizations like Hester Street Collaborative, the Clemente Soto Vélez Cultural and Educational Center, and the Two Bridges Neighborhood Council.

The Little Free Library watched over by Two Bridges, called *Word Play,* is a clever trilingual homage to the diversity of the East River neighborhood. "Two Bridges and I wanted to celebrate and capture the multicultural character of the community and convey the word *library* in Chinese, Spanish, and English," says

designer Chat Travieso. "I decided to use layered plywood to create a visual effect that allows this message, which is painted on the surface of the wood, to change languages based on the angle one views the Library. The edges of the stacked plywood also allude to the vertical patterns produced by books on a bookshelf." Travieso got the community involved with the construction of the Library, holding workshops with youth from the Two Bridges After School Program to choose colors, trace letters, and paint the Library.

Word Play faces the East River waterfront and includes seating so people can stay to read, share with their neighbors, and enjoy the view. "The Library became an important social space in the neighborhood, and was so beloved by the locals that it was constantly renewing itself," says Kerri Culhane, associate director of Two Bridges.

Interested in adding one of these small-scale architectural gems to your urban landscape? Construction plans—generously provided by the designers, the PEN World Voices Festival, and the Architectural League of New York—are available online (see "Connect with Little Free Library" on page 224 for the web address).

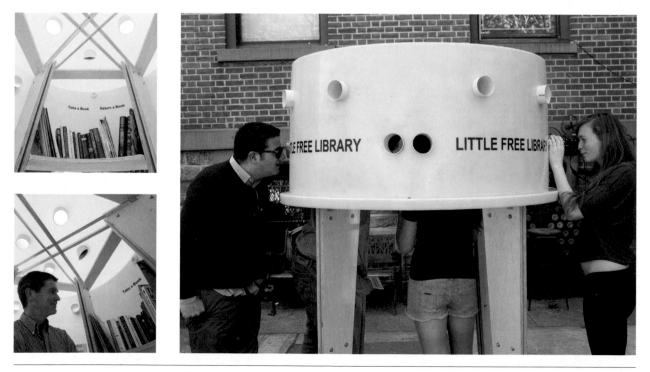

MARGRET ALDRICH

little free library

2015: The Little Free Library returns and redist
Bibliotequita Libre 小型免費圖書館 Littl

MIKE HAEG

Mount Holly, Minnesota, USA

Charter Number: 3570

"More people should think about adding their own homemade publications to their Library. It's a great feeling to have your neighbors reading a comic book you may have drawn or even a small newspaper you've edited."

—MIKE HAEG

Every town needs a Little Free Library, no matter what the community's size. They're popular from sprawling cities like Los Angeles to dots on the map where everybody knows your name. But the tiniest town to host a Little Free Library has to be the self-made city of Mount Holly, Minnesota, population four.

Mount Holly is Minnesota's smallest town, founded by artist Mike Haeg within the city limits of Shakopee (a Twin Cities suburb) in 2003. Mount Holly is just one of Haeg's innovative creations—he's also made things like a hand-knitted scarf big enough to be worn by eighty-nine people at once and a pistol-shaped Bluetooth earpiece. His town of Mount Holly is home to only one family: Haeg; his wife, Tammy Dahlke; and their two kids, Jackson and Autumn. Haeg plays a lot of roles in the microtown, serving as mayor, justice of the peace, and Little Free Librarian. (Jackson heads up the Department of Sanitation, i.e., taking out the trash.)

"It's our mission to provide the highest quality of life to our citizens and to those who visit our fair city," says Haeg, with tongue in cheek. "We believe that arts and music are essential to a healthy community. And our primary export is in making the lives of our friends and neighbors interesting." In addition to stewarding a Little Free Library, Mount Holly hosts events like euchre tournaments, a city festival with pinewood derby races (on the first Saturday in August), an occasional pop-up art gallery, and an international film festival (on the first Saturday in October).

When asked why he established Mount Holly, Haeg says, "It was started at a time when my wife and I moved from the big city, where we had quite a few friends, to the rural suburb in which we grew up, where there wasn't a whole lot going on. By creating the city, with its mission and events, we provided our city friends a reason to come out and visit, and we helped to make life in the suburbs a bit more interesting."

Haeg's Little Free Library, which acts as the public library for the city of four, is built from cedar, with a shake roof and antique hardware. "Our most notable feature is the copper and glass night-light, which is solar powered and pops on only after the sun begins to set," Haeg says.

The town isn't big enough to have its own zip code, but it does have its own newspaper, the *Mount Holly Register*, written and laid out by Haeg himself. There is a second door on the Library where passersby can pick up a free copy of the satirical paper, which bears headlines like "Local Tire Acquitted of Armed Robbery Charges."

"The morning after we erected our Library, I caught a view of two 'tweenage' girls walking down the sidewalk, side by side, each reading their own copy of the newspaper," Haeg says. "More people should think about adding their own homemade

publications to their Library. It's a great feeling to have your neighbors reading a comic book you may have drawn or even a small newspaper you've edited."

![library icon]

FUNDING YOUR LIBRARY

Concerned you don't have enough money to start a Little Free Library? Take heart. With the support available from a variety of sources, your Library can become a reality sooner than you might think.

■ Contact individuals in your neighborhood who share your interest in growing a stronger community—perhaps you know them from a book club, coffee shop, or community garden. They can donate a few dollars, help you find resources, or even become "costewards" who assist in all aspects of the Little Free Library.

■ Approach your local neighborhood association, city council, chamber of commerce, churches, schools, parent groups, and small businesses. They want to see your neighborhood thrive, too. If these groups can't donate money, they may be able to offer building supplies or volunteer labor.

■ Launch a campaign on a crowdfunding website like Kickstarter, Indiegogo, or Razoo. As you read in Sarah Maxey's story on page 39, this can be a very

effective tool to raise money. (Just don't count on the same record-breaking results.)

■ Ask your place of employment if they can help. Many companies are happy to fund community outreach projects like Little Free Libraries. They may even want to get involved in a larger capacity, hosting a team-building event to construct several Little Libraries for the community.

■ Ask large retail stores if they offer funding for local programs. Big-box stores like Target, Walmart, Home Depot, and Lowes often set aside money for community causes. It's good publicity for them and good luck for you.

■ Inquire with your local Girl Scout troop, Boy Scout troop, Lions Club, high school shop class, college architecture department, arts organization, woodworkers' guild, or other similar organization. They might be looking for an interesting project to work on, and your Little Free Library could be it. High schooler James Copeland of Wichita, Kansas, for example, built a Little Free Library as his Eagle Scout project.

If those ideas don't provide what you need, apply for support through Little Free Library's GIFT (Give It Forward Team) Fund, which helps cover the cost of building supplies and registration. An application is available online.

CAROLYN BANCROFT

Bogotá, Colombia

Charter Number: 3254

The first Little Free Library in South America sits on a quiet, cobbled pedestrian street tucked away in the metropolis of Bogotá—Colombia's largest city—and has quickly become a local treasure. So much so that it's guarded (if unofficially) twenty-four hours a day. Here, steward Carolyn Bancroft tells us how it came to be.

Why did you want to bring a Little Free Library to Bogotá?

Bogotá is a literary capital. Among the many projects that are promoted in these parts is the nonprofit People and Stories/Gente y Cuentos [which aims to share literature with those who have little access]. It had its origins in Bogotá in the fifties, when founder Sarah Hirshmann lived here. Coming full circle, it was one of People and Stories' most active supporters who told me about Little Free Libraries.

The idea immediately struck me as a worthwhile project for our neighborhood for a variety of reasons: The small neighborhood is notable in Bogotá for its sense of community; there are an abundance of books (and academics) residing here already; our neighborhood is mixed in its socioeconomic demographics; the city at large promotes reading; and it has a world-renowned public library system. Mostly, it just seemed like a fun idea.

Tell us about your Little Free Library. What makes it special?

We had the box made by carpenters who work for a nonprofit that teaches skills to displaced youngsters and who donated their labor. The decoration is very simple: We painted the box red, green, and yellow. It is situated on a street that is actually a staircase, and it hangs from a stone wall next to a security guard stand.

We didn't place the Little Free Library there because it is guarded, but it does help (the whole box could be lifted). It has been great to see the guards occasionally taking books—although some neighbors may say that it's a distraction from their duties.

What books are in your Little Free Library right now?

We received an amazing donation of *all* the Nobel laureates translated into Spanish. I plan to put them out in small batches, in chronological order, and to use a little publicity via a community blog to get folks interested. The children's books that have been placed in the Library have indeed disappeared quickly. We also have a handful of English-language novels, which surprisingly don't move very quickly. It's surprising to me because anything published in English is costly here.

How has the Library had an impact on your community?

Our neighborhood is unique in Bogotá: it is a small haven in a hectic city and has a distinct bohemian feel. The Little Free Library adds to our character, and I think neighbors are very proud of it.

We did a bit of word-of-mouth promotion for the Library and the typical reaction was, "But the books will all disappear!" This was an expected reaction in a city known for its "take what you can get" persona and high levels of petty crime. We dutifully replied that it wouldn't matter. The surprise is that quite the opposite has occurred: it's hard to convince people to take books! Often I see people gazing in curiosity at our Little Free Library, reading the sign, gaining understanding of the concept, and even exclaiming what a good idea, but not touching the door—much less removing a book. When I encourage them, they typically respond, "But I don't have anything to put inside." Take a book anyway, I tell them. Among our most loyal readers, of course, are our security guards.

The motivation for starting a Little Free Library is, most often, a healthy admiration for novels, nonfiction, and everything bookish. For DooSun You, it was that, plus a random internet search.

DooSun loves spending time in libraries, and says, "When I am in a library, sometimes I forget how much time is passing." One day, when the bibliophile absentmindedly googled the word *library*—for no good reason—the Little Free Library website came up, and he was hooked.

"As soon as I saw it, I wanted to join the Little Free Library movement, because I totally agreed with its purpose," DooSun says. He searched Little Free Library's world map and scoured the internet to try to find a Little Library to visit nearby, but there were none in Korea, so he decided to build his own.

After DooSun installed the Library in front of his apartment and filled it with Korean novels, biographies, and comic books, it took several weeks before the first patron took a book. People simply didn't know what it was. To help explain the Little Free Library concept, DooSun included a QR code on the front of his Library that linked to a dedicated Facebook page, so passersby could use their smartphones to learn more.

DooSun believes that Little Free Libraries will catch on in Korea. "Little Free Libraries make people more social. They awaken the value of sharing. And books are one of the most valuable things," he says. DooSun is helping spread the word and has installed two more Little Libraries. "I thought my first Library was insufficient," he says. "I wanted to build more wonderful Little Free Libraries like other stewards have built."

LAUNCHING YOUR LIBRARY

You've spent hours deciding which Little Free Library you wanted to build or buy. You've pored over paint samples and decorative doodads. You've secured the perfect spot to erect your Library. Now that it's up, how do you encourage people to use it?

■ Invite your neighborhood to a ribbon-cutting ceremony for your Little Free Library, either by word of mouth or a simple flyer. Ask everyone to bring a book and a buck to help keep the new Library stocked. Serve champagne and sparkling cider at the celebration, and be sure to take lots of photos.

■ Write a press release and send it to your local newspapers, radio stations, websites, and television stations. They may want to share your story and promote your Library in the process, especially if there is something unique about your LFL.

■ Make bookmarks with the details of your Little Free Library—where it is, what it is, and how to use it—and stick them in the front doors of your neighbors. (They'll be better received than takeout menus, I promise.) Or give away the bookmarks in your Library.

■ Create a Facebook page for your Little Free Library. Post a note in your Library to invite patrons to "like" the page—or post a QR code that links to your page—so they can stay connected with what's happening at their local Little Free Library. You can post photos of what books are in your Library, send out a call when you need new books, share book news and reviews, and more.

■ Use sidewalk chalk to advertise your Little Free Library. Draw arrows and hopscotch grids, along with LFL information and your favorite book quotes, to lead people from surrounding blocks to your Library.

ELLEN AND COL CSEKE

Calgary, Alberta, Canada

Charter Number: 4840

For sweethearts Ellen and Col Cseke, starting a Little Free Library together led to much more, when Col used the Library as his wingman in a surprise marriage proposal. A wedding soon followed, with the Little Library again playing a part. Here, the Csekes share their story.

What is your Little Free Library's story? Why did you decide to build it, and what makes it special?

We knew we wanted a Little Free Library after hearing about one that a friend of Ellen's mother had built. She had such beautiful stories of strangers knocking on her door to chat about books and countless other interactions with fellow book-lovers. We both love reading and community building, so it seemed like a perfect fit, and we talked about building one together.

Then, while Ellen was away for a month working in another city, Col secretly built the Library and had Ellen's sister cover it in portraits of reading dinosaurs. Col picked Ellen up from the airport, and when they pulled up to the house, there sat the shiny new Little Free Library on their lawn.

Inside was a single book. On the cover Col had typed his marriage proposal. He had hollowed out the middle of the book to hold a ring box. Unfortunately, Ellen was so taken with the Little Library that it took her awhile to realize he was proposing!

We were married in September 2013, and the Little Free Library was a big part of our wedding ceremony, which our friends wrote and performed. Because of the Library's role in our engagement story and our shared love of reading and community, it was treated as a sort of "altar." Our friends wrote:

> Our altar is this Little Free Library. For Ellen and Col built and curate this library themselves. In fact, in the week preceding the wedding, there were more photos of people visiting their lawn library than nuptial anxieties. It is a microcosm of the way they operate in the world.
>
>   They seek that which will challenge their assumptions. They get excited about the world being revealed in a new way and generously share that excitement. The library brings together different communities, as these two people bring us together today. So before this altar of expansive thought, expansive love, we find our two humble heroes.

The rings were presented in a hollowed-out book—*Lord of the Rings,* cheekily.

What meaningful, surprising, or bizarre interactions have happened because of your Little Free Library?

One morning Ellen looked out the window and saw a woman and a five-year-old girl stop at the Library. While her mom browsed the books, the little one pulled out a "how to do yoga" book. She plopped the book down and started doing yoga poses on the front lawn.

Late one night, Ellen was standing outside the front door looking for her keys. From behind her she heard a gruff voice calling, "Hey, hey you, excuse me." She saw a rather rough-looking guy standing on the sidewalk and nervousness went through her body; it was dark and no one else was out. Then the gentleman asked, "Hey, I have a ton of books—if the Library is too full, can I leave a box beside it with the extras that don't fit?"

And we had a good laugh one day when a canvasser who knocked on our door expressed concern that someone might "steal" a book. How can you steal something that's free?

What books are in your Little Free Library right now?

Lots of novels, like *Happiness* by Will Ferguson and *A Thousand Splendid Suns* by Khaled Hosseini; textbooks and how-tos: *Biology of the Invertebrates, Japanese Phrases for Dummies, What to Expect When You're Expecting*; and a few *Reader's Digest* anthologies.

How has your Little Free Library had an impact on your community?

This summer, we had a wonderful conversation with a woman who pulled up in her car to do a book swap. She asked us about the Library, and the sweetest point was when she told us that she had lost the habit of reading for the past few years, but having the Library in her neighborhood had started her reading again, and now she's in and out of our yard every other week.

In addition, we've discovered books that we would have never signed out of the "real" library or found in a bookstore, including a lot of great new Canadian novels.

Beyond these individual experiences, the Library has given strangers permission to talk to one another. It's a bright yellow icebreaker for the neighborhood.

Do you have any advice for new LFL stewards?

We see the Little Free Library as something that belongs to the community. We've met dog walkers who have changed their routes so that they pass it every day. To start, we did our best to decorate it in a very engaging and approachable way, and we made sure it was very well stocked, and with that strong start, it's been entirely low maintenance from there.

Whenever we think, "Oh, it's getting low, I'll go pull some books," more show up in an hour or two. Or when it gets totally full, people take out more books.

One other little note: We rent the house we live in, so we weren't able to pound the base into the lawn. Instead we just built a wooden base that is weighed down with sandbags. You could do the same in an apartment lobby, a parking lot, or just about anywhere.

![house icon]

IF YOU BUILD IT

Constructing your own Little Free Library can be a hugely rewarding experience: you get to decide every detail, from size and shape to color and style. Think of it as your dream house, without the mortgage.

Anyone can build a Little Free Library, so don't let the task intimidate you. Founder Todd Bol is the first to point out that he was a simple hobbyist when he built the first one in 2009 (and it's still standing). Below are tips and tricks to inspire you to grab some tools and get started.

■ Builders have made Little Free Libraries to reflect their hobbies, interests, collections, occupations, families, or home states. Now it's time for you to use your imagination. For ideas and inspiration, visit the photo galleries on Little Free Library's Pinterest, Flickr, and Instagram pages.

■ Use recycled materials when you can. Some of the repurposed materials Bol has used include barn wood, garage doors, deck railings, doghouses, rulers, and discarded materials from building sites. (Be sure to ask before you take anything that's not yours.)

■ Build your Little Free Library to last. Use paints or stains made for exterior use (interior paints will not survive the elements) and finish the Library with several coats of sealer. If you're not sure what kind of paint or sealer to buy, ask for recommendations from the folks at your local hardware store.

■ Safety first: to protect visitors to your Library, use plexiglass on the door rather than real glass, never use lead paint, and be sure to sand or file off any rough edges on wood or metal.

■ Be sure to save a bit of paint for touch-ups. Once your Little Free Library starts getting a lot of use, the latch and door may need to be freshened up now and then with a quick sweep of paint. And note that your entire Library may benefit from a fresh coat of paint and sealer every year or so.

MARGRET ALDRICH

- Join the Neighborhood Library Builders page on Facebook, where Little Free Library builders share advice, ideas, and photos.

- See the appendix for sample Little Free Library plans, building instructions, and directions for mounting your Library, or visit littlefreelibrary.org.

Build Community

USING LITTLE FREE LIBRARIES TO COME TOGETHER

"I have found that among its other benefits, giving liberates the soul of the giver."

—MAYA ANGELOU

CHAPTER 3
BUILD COMMUNITY

"I've met more people in the last seven days than I have in the last ten years," is a common refrain from new Little Free Library stewards. It's true: the Libraries subtly but surely bring people together. They shine a light on common interests, provide a conversation starter beyond weather patterns or game scores, and most importantly—they offer a reason to pause and connect.

This kind of community building is what Robert Putnam, author of *Bowling Alone: The Collapse and Revival of American Community,* has lamented the modern world is missing: the instinct to get together for a pickup basketball game, share food at a potluck, commiserate over the poker table, or happily accommodate the neighbor at the door asking to borrow a cup of sugar. A Little Free Library can help grease our social wheels, establishing bonds by serving as a miniature "third place"—a neutral, public space outside of work and home—to invigorate our communities in the same way a local coffee shop or familiar bar might.

A Little Free Library isn't a cup of sugar on the sidewalk, and it isn't a corner pub, but it broadcasts that same message of welcome with a quiet ease. It's a chance for neighbors to share with neighbors, to give something of yourself, and to engage with your community, one sweet book at a time. Here, read how stewards are using their Little Free Libraries to connect with neighbors, and learn how effortless—and enjoyable—community building can be.

MELANIE PETERSON-NAFZIGER

Saint Paul, Minnesota, USA

Charter Number: 7830

MELEAH MAYNARD AND MIKE HOIUM

Minneapolis, Minnesota, USA

Charter Number: 5897

A Chinese proverb says that a book is like a garden carried in the pocket. Twin Cities stewards Melanie Peterson-Nafziger and Meleah Maynard want to share that garden in every way they can. Both use their respective Little Free Libraries to bring neighbors together through shared books and shared seeds.

Featuring a lush and tangled garden on the roof, and a community seed exchange in a salvaged drawer, Peterson-Nafziger's Little Library is a welcoming

MARGRET ALDRICH

presence in her St. Paul neighborhood. "I love to share great books with people," she says, "and I also loved the whimsical nature of installing an artful element (the LFL) on the edge of our private property. I like the space it creates for people who wouldn't otherwise meet each other to get into a conversation. And I like how Little Free Libraries blur the lines between public and private space. Installing a Little Free Library is one step toward opening our lives to others."

The top shelf of this library is for sharing garden seeds in spring and fall.

Instructions inside.

The entire Library—from the lumber to the roof to the finishing materials— is made from reused junk: The aluminum cans were scavenged from people's recycling bins. The door is an old basement window. The handles are old window pulls. And the green roof materials are leftovers from bigger projects.

"We planted the green roof with violets that we dug out of our yard. We like that the roof will burst into bloom in spring and will then be covered with the heart-shaped leaves of the violets throughout the summer," says Peterson-Nafziger. To make sure the books stay dry when the rooftop garden is watered, she created a gasket that keeps water from leaking in by adhering an old bike inner tube to the inside edge of the door.

The violet-topped Little Free Library holds books like Barbara Kingsolver's *The Bean Trees*, Robert McNair's *Basic River Canoeing*, and *American Indian Prose and Poetry* in the main compartment, as well as seeds for chives, buttercups, and dill in the seed-swap drawer, which Peterson-Nafziger built from old oak flooring. "We also included a bulletin board on the inside of the Library where people can post messages and info they'd like to share with the neighborhood. It's always fun to find a new message there," she says.

Across the Mississippi River in south Minneapolis, master gardener and gardening blogger Meleah Maynard is also growing community with her Little Free Library book and seed exchange. Maynard's Library has two shelves, with the top one devoted to seed sharing in the spring and fall. "I've got lots of seeds from my own gardens, and because I write a blog and gardening column for the local neighborhood paper, it was easy to spread the word that people were welcome to take some and drop off their own seeds," Maynard says.

In no time, the Library was stocked with all sorts of annual, perennial, and vegetable seeds, including lacinato kale, red-swamp milkweed, Queen Anne's lace, black-eyed Susan, morning glory, datura, blackberry lily, and more. Maynard keeps the seed exchange organized by leaving paper envelopes and plastic bags above the books, so visitors can label their seeds for the next neighbor who stops by.

"People gather around Little Free Libraries to talk and share books, and now seeds," Maynard says. "At a time when we're all busy and racing around, I feel like it creates a sense of belonging to a neighborhood or even a tribe of people who love books as much as someone else does. It makes me happy to share that."

HOW TO START A LITTLE SEED LIBRARY

Sharing seeds is another wonderful way to connect with your neighbors, and a Little Free Library is the perfect spot to do it. Follow these simple steps to start a seed exchange in your Little Library.

■ Post a notice on your Little Free Library that invites neighbors to share seeds. Leave envelopes and pencils inside so that visitors can add seeds to the envelopes and label what they are. Do they have growing tips to share? Those can be written on the envelopes as well.

Please reserve the top shelf for sharing seeds in the spring and fall.

■ If seeds are for vegetables, herbs, or fruits, encourage donors to include several copies of their favorite recipe that features the ingredient, along with the story behind it.

■ At the end of the growing season, gather your fellow seed exchangers for a potluck—featuring the best of their garden bounty—at a local park or your backyard. Trade stories about garden successes or failures, share new recipes you discovered, and talk about what you'd like to grow next year. If anyone needs help with garden cleanup or other yard work, sign up volunteers.

■ Extra credit: Find out if there is an Eat for Equity (eatforequity.org) chapter in your area. This organization—which promotes community building and a culture of generosity through shared meals—is teaming up with Little Free Library to launch an heirloom recipe and seed library series.

COTTON BRYAN

Chapel Hill, North Carolina, USA

Charter Number: 10887

English teacher and school principal Cotton Bryan uses his visually striking Little Free Library and a shared sketchbook to reenergize a sense of community within his Chapel Hill, North Carolina, neighborhood.

What is your Little Free Library's story? Why did you decide to build it, and what makes it special?
My family and I read about the movement in *Our State* magazine and just knew right away that we needed to be a part of it. We have a lot of folk art in our home—some of which includes bottle caps—so our kids chose bottle caps as our motif when we started designing. There are 684 bottle caps individually nailed to the outside of the Library.

What meaningful interactions have happened because of your Little Free Library?
Within the first few weeks, we were amazed by how many interactions with walkers and neighbors the Little Free Library facilitated. It instantly generated a lot of positive energy and goodwill in the neighborhood.

How has the Library had an impact on your community?
I think a lot about the second law of thermodynamics, which basically says that in a closed system, things will tend toward disorder and chaos unless you input new energy into the system. I see the Little Free Library as one little way we're inputting new energy into the community of our neighborhood. It's one force added in the direction of creating and strengthening community.

What ideas do you have for using your Little Free Library to build community?
We had an official grand opening that was a celebration of books, community, and Krispy Kreme doughnuts. I collected all these famous quotations about reading and books, printed them on leaflets, and guests got to shout out the quotations.

We invited the whole neighborhood and others to the party. At the bottom of the invite we printed, "Optional: bring one great book to contribute to the library."

We also have three community art books in our Library that circulate. These are sketchbooks that borrowers take home, use one to three pages for their art, then return to the Library for others to contribute. Over time you can see art from all over the neighborhood and town.

LIEKE PLOEGER

The Hague, South Holland, Netherlands

Charter Number: 4932

> *"I strongly believe in the rising power of the gift economy. I think it makes people happier to share their belongings"*

—LIEKE PLOEGER

As part of a Little Free Library's natural affinity for promoting stronger communities, it promotes a gift economy as well—one where trading resources trumps buying more, more, more. Here, Lieke Ploeger tells us how her Library inspires her community to connect and share with each other, offline and online.

What is it about Little Free Library that grabbed your interest?

I've always loved books and reading. After completing a master's in modern Western literature, I worked for the National Library of the Netherlands for several years. Currently I'm working as community manager for the Open Knowledge Foundation, helping to promote free and open access to the digital cultural heritage held by galleries, libraries, archives, and museums. So apart from spreading a love of books, the community-building part around a Little Free Library is something that interests me a lot, too.

In addition, I strongly believe in the rising power of the gift economy. I think it makes people happier to share their belongings (and receive from others in return) than to always strive to make more money and buy more stuff. From my book collection, a large part was always loaned to friends, and I began to prefer a smaller, rotating book collection instead of a house chock-full of books that are usually just standing on the shelf collecting dust.

Finally, I love street art and see Little Free Libraries as an extension of this as well.

What is your Little Free Library's story? Why did you decide to build it, and what makes it special?

The idea of starting a Little Free Library appealed to me for various reasons: it stimulates reading (the barrier to picking up a book becomes very low, and people who already read a lot can discover interesting new books in this way); it builds community in the neighborhood (it gets people talking to each other more); it just brightens up the street; and it shows people an alternative to the ever-growing commercialization of the public space (so many advertisements telling us to buy more and more stuff are everywhere around us). Especially now in times of economic crisis, I think it's great if people share more of what they have.

It was also a sort of experiment for me: I thought to just put it up and see what happened. In my neighborhood, I came across a perfect space to put the Little Free Library: next to a doggy park and close to a busy street crossing, there was a small bench with an empty space next to it. I found a suitable little wooden cupboard online (secondhand), painted it in bright colors (so that it looked nicer, but also so that people would find it too beautiful to vandalize), made it water-proof with an extra roof and some waterproof varnish (essential with the Dutch climate), and collected around thirty books (a mix of children's books, novels in Dutch and English, travel books, and some cookbooks).

On February 3, 2013, I put it up and also created a Facebook page on the same day. Within the first week, we had two hundred followers, [coverage on] some local blogs, radio interviews, and an article in a local Dutch newspaper. The pub-licity just kept growing after that, and books have been changing hands quickly ever since!

How has the Library had an impact on your community?

The Little Free Library has been a big success in my neighborhood; I often see people there talking to each other about the books in it, which is great. Very important to me is that by putting up an LFL, you show people that they are able to make their neighborhood better, and that they can take the initiative for this—they don't need to wait for someone else, or go through all kinds of trouble to get permissions.

What is the weirdest book (or other item) that has shown up in your Little Free Library?

One day last summer, somebody put a little stuffed heart on our Library with the text "I love you," which was very sweet. Somebody else donated a book that he wrote, on the very day of publication, so we had it as a first edition! For the new year, I made a collection full of new age inspirational books (Buddhism, Zen, Deepak Chopra, shamanism, and so on)—but also added a photography book of men's underwear: *De onderbroek* by Birgit Engel.

Do you have any advice for new Little Free Library stewards?

I think the most important thing is choosing a good place somewhere where enough people see it, and where they have some space around to stand still and have a look at the books.

As for community building, I've found that Facebook works great. I regularly update my page (at least three times a week) with stories of other Little Free Libraries, photos of the current content of the Library, news related to other initiatives where people give/share their stuff (we have, for example, a cupboard like an LFL in Holland where people share food items), and interesting or funny content related to reading. And of course I also support all other Little Free Libraries that are on Facebook—with some, I am in regular contact.

Last summer I moved to Berlin, so now I'm managing my LFL from a distance (though sometimes I come back to check it). This works fine. Due to my large number of Facebook fans, I always know what's going on, and I can contact someone from my network if something is needed.

MARGRET ALDRICH

EXPLORE THE NEIGHBORHOOD

Gather friends and neighbors to celebrate Little Free Libraries in action, beyond your front yard.

■ Plan a bike tour of local Little Free Libraries with your neighbors. Visit the global map online to find nearby Libraries or simply keep an eye out for LFLs in your area. Design a route that takes you by the Libraries, then print out or draw a map. Make copies, gather friends and neighbors, then bike from location to location, leaving a book and a note for the stewards in every Library you drop by.

■ Write clues to send friends and neighbors on a bookish scavenger hunt around your city. Stops could include the public library, your favorite bookshop, or other Little Free Libraries in the area. The final clue should lead them back to your Library. The first one back collects a prize and everyone socializes in your backyard.

■ Take a field trip to a secondhand bookstore. Post a notice of the date and time of the field trip in your Little Free Library, then carpool, walk, or cycle to the store with your neighbors. Ask everyone to search the stacks for their favorite books, and then reconvene to talk about the titles everyone chose.

■ "Borrow" a favorite item from a friend, partner, or kid—a stuffed animal or garden gnome would be good choices—then photo bomb Little Free Libraries all over your city using the item. It can be inside the Library, sitting atop it, or peeking from behind. E-mail the pictures to the object's owner, who will get a kick out of seeing all the Libraries their beloved object has visited.

■ Keep an eye out for an upcoming author reading that you'd like to attend. Add a few books by that author to your Little Free Library, and invite visitors to join you at the event. Be sure to gather for discussion (and maybe a drink) afterwards.

AARP AND LITTLE BROTHERS— FRIENDS OF THE ELDERLY

Minneapolis, Minnesota, USA

Charter Number: Multiple

When older adults become isolated, loneliness sets in, quality of life declines, and serious health issues can result, says Jay Haapala, associate director of community outreach for AARP Minnesota. "Research shows that the chances of slips and falls all the way to diabetes, cancer, and other negative health impacts are much higher when folks are isolated from their families and from their neighbors."

Little Free Libraries are a wonderful way for elders to get to know people in their communities and lead happier lives. To that end, Little Free Library's Friends through the Years initiative is bringing Libraries to seniors' front yards with funds provided by the AARP Foundation and partnerships with Lutheran Social Services, the Wilder Foundation, retirement communities, and organizations like Little

MARGRET ALDRICH

Brothers–Friends of the Elderly (LBFE), a national organization that pairs volunteers with older adults to help combat the loneliness that often comes with aging.

The program is getting cheers from elders in the Twin Cities, where twenty Little Free Libraries are being installed by LBFE and AARP Minnesota. One of the first recipients of a Little Library was a gentleman named Denis, who has already experienced the positive effects. "I'm really excited to share my books about the supernatural with my neighbors, and find out what things they're interested in, too," he says.

"A Little Free Library helps to combat isolation by getting the elder to watch their Library for familiar faces and in nice weather sit outside and converse with neighbors who stop by to take a book and later return a book," says Sandy O'Donnell, LBFE's program services director. For someone who lives alone, connections like these can be lifesaving. "The conversations lead to our elders getting to know their neighbors—which of course relieves isolation. They have a reason, as the steward of the Library, to go outside and make sure there are plenty of books and to see if there are new ones for them to read."

By tending a Little Free Library, older adults open themselves to the warmth of their communities, and they are rarely disappointed. "When a Little Free Library pops up, the neighbors come out and take a look—and they get to know one another on the curbside," says Haapala. "It's almost as simple as that—the likelihood that they will meet their neighbors is much better. And also, perhaps, they're more likely to get some help raking the leaves, or some help shoveling snow—or just have a friend."

AMY WALTON AND JAMES GARRETT

Dallas, Texas, USA

Charter Number: 7524

When Amy met James on an online dating site, she didn't expect Little Free Libraries and Stephen Colbert to be part of their modern romance. But LFLs don't only bring readers and books together—they can bring people together, too.

On their first date, pop artist James told Amy about a project he'd started to give away free pieces of artwork in an alley between the 1800 and 1900 blocks of Henderson Avenue in Dallas, Texas. Visitors to the Artbot138 Gallery could

take home screen-printed, spray-painted artworks at no charge. Amy loved the idea and told James about her obsession with Little Free Libraries—a similar concept, but with books.

On their second date, Amy packed a lunch, and she and James spent five hours driving around North Texas visiting Little Free Libraries. "That day, he told me he'd build one for me," she says.

After a few more months of dating, they took the big leap—not getting married, but launching the Cedar Springs Heights Little Free Library in Amy's front yard. It was a team effort that reflects their love of art and collaboration: "James built a great box that had removable panels, so we can change out the art. The first art panels I created from mod-podging pieces of sixties magazines. We plan to invite other artist friends to create future designs."

James moved in not long after, and the two take care of the Little Free Library together. They started a Facebook page (facebook.com/CedarSprings HeightsFreeLibrary) to share quirky, bookish news and have thrown parties centered around the Library. "We hosted a book swap in conjunction with my

MARGRET ALDRICH

annual Halloween party, riffing with an 'All Hallow's Read' theme," Amy says. "All of our friends went home with new books, and we had a pile to funnel into the Library."

In addition to their commitment to each other, Amy and James are committed to being friends to their community. They've even gotten television host and comedian Stephen Colbert involved. "We live in an urban neighborhood that is very diverse, and one of our goals has been to ensure our books reflect the cultures and languages of our neighbors," Amy says. "This fall, I petitioned Stephen Colbert of *The Colbert Report* to provide some items we could auction to help purchase Spanish-language kids' books and to help provide seed money to others to build Little Free Libraries in other neighborhoods that could benefit." Colbert responded with autographed books—a fitting contribution for their fundraising auction.

GROUP PROJECTS

Use your Little Free Library as a catalyst for growing community—choose one or more of these prompts to try with your neighbors.

■ Write a story together, round robin–style. You come up with the first paragraph, introducing a setting and a character or two, and then leave the story in your Little Free Library with instructions that others should add to it. When it's done, host a public reading at your Library. You might not create the next Great American Novel, but you're sure to end up with something memorable. (Try a community screenplay, poem, or children's book, too.)

■ Make your Little Free Library the neighborhood watercooler. Add a bulletin board or chalkboard to the side of your Library where people can post upcoming events, notices, pictures of lost dogs, notes of celebration, or whatever news they want to share with neighbors. Is your school having a fundraiser? Are you a musician with an upcoming show? Promote it here. And make it known that loitering at the Little Library is encouraged.

■ Pick a day for your Little Free Library to become a Little Free Gallery: Invite people to bring artworks—paintings, prints, small sculptures, and so on—that they want to give away or trade. These can be professional or homemade. Finish that art project that's been languishing in your basement, and be amazed at the masterpieces your neighbors had hidden away.

■ Leave a notebook in your Little Free Library with questions to get to know your neighbors better. You could ask reader-related questions like, "What

book changed your life?" "When do you find time to read?" and "What was your favorite book as a kid?" or community-related questions like, "How long have you lived in the area?" "What is the best change that has happened over the years here?" and "What do you think we can do to make our neighborhood stronger?" After a month or two, make it more personal by inviting Library visitors to meet at your house or a local coffee shop to talk about the questions you've posed.

■ Host a children's book swap at your Little Free Library. Ask all the kids in your neighborhood to dress as their favorite book characters and to bring a few books they've outgrown to trade with other young readers. (Kids are crackerjack negotiators and barterers, so the swap could get lively.) Read a book aloud to them, or let them read aloud to each other.

■ Get to know a senior citizen or two in your neighborhood—especially those who might not be able to walk to your Little Free Library. Find out what their favorite genre is. If a book shows up in your Library that looks as if it might interest them, deliver it to their door. If they want to return it to the Little Library when they're done, ask them to tell you their minireview; transcribe it and include it inside the book.

■ Start a perpetual game of book trivia. Post a question in your Little Free Library like, "Where was poet Ron Padgett born?" or "What is the name of Nancy Drew's boyfriend?" Whoever is the first to write down the correct answer gets to come up with the next trivia question and wins a free book. (Of course, everyone always wins a free book at a Little Free Library.)

■ Invite your neighbors to redecorate your Little Free Library. Pick a day for the LFL facelift, then provide paint, collaging materials, or decorative additions like bottle caps or Scrabble tiles to spruce it up. If you want your neighbors to make their mark more literally, ask them to add their handprints or paint their names on the Library.

LARISSA KYZER

Reykjavík, Iceland

Charter Number: 2896

Iceland's only Little Free Library sits in Hjólmskalagarður, a park next to the pond in the center of Reykjavík. It was installed there by Larissa Kyzer as a thank-you to the city she adopted after moving there from New York. Her hope was that the Library would foster a feeling of community and literary excitement, and she hasn't been disappointed.

What is your Little Free Library's story? Why did you decide to build it, and what makes it special?

Little Free Library Reykjavík (LFLR), or Lítil Bókhlaða in Icelandic, is the very first Little Free Library in Iceland. As a librarian and avid reader, I've always loved the Little Free Library project and felt that it would be particularly appropriate for Iceland, a country with a rich literary tradition and vibrant reading culture.

I moved to Iceland in 2012 when I received a Fulbright/Árni Magnusson Institute grant to study Icelandic at the University of Iceland. (I hope to one day become a literary translator and translate Icelandic fiction into English.) I felt that bringing the first Little Free Library to Iceland would be fitting way to give back to a literary culture that has meant a great deal to me, and would also be a great way to become more involved with the literary community here in Reykjavík.

I envisioned LFLR as a community-building project, and it was really very successful in this respect. I funded the project through a crowdsourcing platform in Iceland and received donations from people in the United States, Iceland, and several other countries, too. All but a very few of the books in the collection were donated by local and foreign publishers, Icelandic authors, and the Reykjavík City Library; the Reykjavík UNESCO City of Literature office helped me get the city permits to install the Library in a public park; a local poet helped to translate all the informational material into Icelandic; a local carpenter helped with the installation project; artists in the U.S. designed and made the fundraising gifts for free; and supportive readers in the community volunteered to become stewards of the Library, keeping an eye on the unit and helping me keep it filled with books.

What meaningful, surprising, or bizarre interactions have happened because of your Little Free Library?

I just recently found out that over the summer, one of the Library stewards received an early morning call one Saturday, telling him that the Library had been vandalized and that he needed to come right away and take a look at it so that a damage report could be filed with the police. Hardly awake, he marched down to the park, absolutely furious that someone would have vandalized the Library. When he got there, his friends jumped out of the bushes (with coffee and a croissant for him) and whisked him off for his bachelor party. The Library was fine, of course, but they all knew that nothing would get him out of bed faster than thinking that something had happened to it!

What books are in your Little Free Library right now?

Since the Library is located in a public park, the LFLR collection is pretty fluid—every time I visit it, there are new and unexpected books that people have left.

When it was first installed, however, the collection included around fifty-five books in a wide variety of languages: English and Icelandic, of course, but also Czech, Danish, Finnish, French, German, Hungarian, Italian, Norwegian, Spanish, Swedish, and many others. The idea was that Reykjavík is actually a pretty multilingual

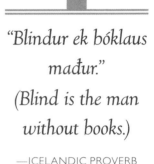

"Blindur ek bóklaus maður."
(Blind is the man without books.)

—ICELANDIC PROVERB

city—Icelanders tend to speak and read in a number of languages, and there is a growing population of immigrants and foreigners as well—and that it would be the most useful to the community to have books available in many languages.

I collected books (novels, knitting manuals, travel guides, kids' books, political commentary, and so on) from a number of publishers in Reykjavík and the U.S., and also received large donations of sci-fi, literary fiction, crime fiction, and more from the Reykjavík City Library, as well as dozens of new translations of Icelandic books from the Icelandic Literature Center. So the first collection was really very diverse.

What is the weirdest book (or other item) that has shown up in your Little Free Library?

One of my favorites was a sci-fi novel that was donated when the Library started. It was called *Earthman's Burden* (by Poul Andersen and Gordon Dickson) and was about a species of space teddy bears who love to act out scenes from Earth history but tend to mix up the historical details. There was also a pretty great Icelandic comic book written, drawn, and self-published by two young local artists about a teenage vampire called Vampíra.

Do you have any construction tips or other advice to share?

The main concern with LFLR was that it be waterproof—Reykjavík is a very wet city! We ordered one of the Amish Shed kits created by Little Free Library and painted it with a waterproof stain. It also had to be mounted on a gigantic concrete anvil so that it wouldn't blow over (Reykjavík is also a very, very windy city), and the anvil—being the kind used by the city for public signage— is bright yellow. It has since been dubbed "Little Yellowstone" and is visible from quite a ways away.

The easiest part of the process for me was getting the books together, because anyone I told about the project was excited to add a book. I'd suggest getting in touch with local publishers and asking for donations, and also contacting the local library to find out if there are any books that they are deaccessioning (getting rid of) that might still be of interest to local readers. Not only do you get a lot of free books this way, you also help to spread the word about your Little Free Library.

You approached your Little Free Library as a community-building project. How has it had an impact on you and your community?

Personally, I've met a lot of people because of the Library. I feel linked to the literary landscape in Reykjavík—the city's literary organizations; local authors, illustrators, and poets; as well as the city's readers—in a way that I wasn't before I started this project. On a broader level, I'm excited by the way that LFLR has reached beyond me and has touched people in the community, and even travelers. I've had people excitedly tell me about the Library on two separate occasions, not knowing that it was my project in the first place. I've received letters (left in the Library) from tourists who were delighted to stumble upon it in the park. I've had authors send me their books (from other countries) to be added to the collection. I wanted LFLR to bring readers of all ages and interests and languages together, and I think it really has.

HARLEM GROWN AND URBAN INNOVATIONS

New York, New York, USA

Charter Number: 7078

Good food and good books blossom in the garden tended by Harlem Grown, a nonprofit organization that inspires healthy, ambitious kids through hands-on lessons in urban farming, sustainability, and nutrition.

"We operate a third-acre urban garden in Central Harlem that is home to many youth programs," says program director Kelly Gillen. "Our garden produces more than five hundred pounds of fresh fruits and vegetables each year." The leafy greens, bright peppers, and other kinds of produce are especially important in an area where fast food restaurants and bodegas vastly outnumber grocery stores. In addition to nurturing healthy kids, the Harlem Grown garden nurtures community and is used as a gathering space for events like film nights, yoga classes, and cookouts.

When another local community group, Urban Innovations, volunteered to install, paint, and maintain a Little Free Library in Harlem Grown's garden, Gillen was thrilled. "Urban Innovations is a group of developmentally disabled Harlem residents who work hard to give back to their community. They are truly an inspirational and giving group, and they volunteer with Harlem Grown throughout the summer," she says.

The Little Free Library designed by Urban Innovations reflects the mix of urban and natural landscapes found at Harlem Grown, with a city skyline on the back and a bee on its roof. Inside, patrons find children's books, farming and gardening books, and health books, such as *The Encyclopedia of Healing Foods* by Michael Murphy, Joseph Pizzorno, and Lara Pizzorno; *Tuttle's Red Barn* by Richard

Michelson and Mary Azarian; *Fletcher and the Springtime Blossoms* by Julia Rawlinson and Tiphanie Beeke; and *The Boy Who Harnessed the Wind* by William Kamkwamba, Bryan Mealer, and Elizabeth Zunon.

"Our students are constantly (and I mean constantly) checking out the books in the Library and sitting in the garden to read," Gillen says. "Urban Innovations keeps the Library fully stocked and rotates in new books every few months. It has been a fantastic addition to our garden space and helps spread the love of reading among our youth."

ROSALIE AND CHRIS STREET

Mount Martha, Victoria, Australia

Charter Number: 10883

Illustrator and artist Rosalie Street thought a Little Free Library would be a good way for her daughters Iris, Lily, and Daisy to learn the value of sharing and a friendly community spirit.

"Projects like this create ripples that make the world a better place," Street says. "I knew we had the perfect neighborhood to make one work. A lot of retired people and young families walk past our house on the way to the park, or if they are walking their dogs around the block. All the neighbors appear to love it, and I've met many neighbors I hadn't spoken to before. It gives people an instant conversation topic and a new destination to walk to."

Beyond the new camaraderie on the block, residents are pleased with the books, which have included *The Magic Pudding* and *Just a Minute* for kids and *Picnic at Hanging Rock* and *My Life as a Fake* for adults. One man told Street that he hadn't read a book in ten years, but since he found their Little Free Library—which has a roof designed to look like a book—he'd read five.

Iris, Lily, and Daisy enjoy leaving little stones and shells around the bottom of the Library for other children in the neighborhood to put in their pockets and take home. The children believe that they're good luck, and if you find one, you can make a wish.

The girls have also received treasures of their own. "One day my girls checked the Little Free Library after school, and the lady across the road had left a parcel wrapped up in brown paper with their names on it," says Street. "She had thoughtfully compiled a selection of books that she knew they would love."

THE STEWARDS' CLUB

Get to know other Little Free Library stewards in your area and around the world.

■ Find a Little Free Library pen pal. Go to the world map on littlefreelibrary. org and explore Little Libraries around the world. Choose a Library that piques your interest, whether for its location or design, and write to the steward. (Many stewards include mailing or e-mail addresses with their world map entry.) Share your experiences as a Little Free Library steward and ask about theirs. Why did they choose to build a Little Library? How did their community respond? What is different about your stories? What is universal?

■ Visit Little Free Libraries when you travel. When you're planning your trip, check the Little Free Library world map to find out which Libraries are near your destination, then stop by when you're in town. If you want to meet the stewards directly, correspond with them in advance to set up an in-person visit. If you can't connect with them, leave a book and a note in their LFL instead. What about their Library inspires you, and how does it differ from others you've seen?

■ Start an inter-LFL loan system by trading books with stewards from another state. Go to the world map again and pick a part of the country that intrigues you. (Stewards Linda Prout and Tracy Mumford traded books between New Orleans and Minneapolis, for example. Read their stories on pages 190 and 144.) Contact the steward you're interested in swapping books with, and suggest that you trade books specific to your region. Examples might include a wine guide from a steward in California or a Carson McCullers novel from a steward in Georgia. Keep in touch to find out how your books were received by their readers.

JAY WALLJASPER

What does it mean to be part of the "commons"? How do Little Free Libraries fit into this idea, boosting the sharing economy and making our neighborhoods better? Here, Jay Walljasper, author of *All That We Share: A Field Guide to the Commons* and senior fellow and editor of onthecommons.org, explores the communal benefits of Little Free Libraries.

Let's talk about the idea of the commons. Can you explain what the commons is and why it should be important to us?

The commons is all that we share—not just things, but also ways of working together. It's a form of ownership where we own together rather than privately. That seems like kind of an exotic idea, but when you stop to think about it, you realize the street in front of your house belongs to everybody. The airwaves that are used for cell phones and radio and television belong to everybody. The internet belongs to everybody. The air and the water. The sky. Parks and libraries and public spaces. Once you start cataloging them, there're actually quite a few things that are absolutely essential for our biological and social and economic survival that really do belong to all of us.

To believe in the commons doesn't mean that you have to essentially be an anarchist and believe that all property is theft. It's just simply making a sound decision on what resources make the most sense to be owned together and what resources make the most sense to be owned privately. And different people will draw those lines in different places.

How do Little Free Libraries contribute to the idea of the commons and stronger communities?

It's interesting, because it's kind of cut and dry that the city water system and the streets belong to everybody, but the commons also interconnects with the things we own privately. If you ask people where's their favorite place to hang out when the community gets together, they may say the coffee shop, the tavern, the bowling alley, the VFW. Those things are technically private. But yet they function very much as commons. There's the concept of public space, but then there's also the concept of semipublic space.

Little Free Libraries fit in with that, because they're usually privately owned, and they're usually on private property, yet at the same time they function as

"Even if no one's there, you feel a greater sense of connection. You kind of have a sense of who the people are who own the house."

—JAY WALLJASPER

commons, because one of the important things that commons do is bring people together. Little Free Libraries are a great thing, because they get books into the hands of people who can use them, but equally important is that they give people a chance to stop, talk, and connect. Even if no one's there, you feel a greater sense of connection. You kind of have a sense of who the people are who own the house—the Libraries are usually decorated in an individualistic way that expresses their personalities. Anything that gets us to be more connected to our surroundings is good, and Little Free Libraries do that.

Little Free Libraries went from one to twenty-five thousand in five years. Why do you think Little Free Libraries have become so popular? What makes people connect with them?

I think it was one of those ideas whose time had come. For most of human history, we lived cheek by jowl with other people, crammed into tenement apartments and shacks and things like that, and there was the Great Dream of having some space to ourselves. I think we succeeded beyond our wildest imaginations—at least many people, particularly in the United States. And I think there's a sense of isolation. Often there's not a coffee shop on the corner, or a tavern on the corner, or a grocery store on the corner anymore. Just to have a Little Free Library there kind of helps personalize what might be a lovely architectural landscape, but that can sometimes seem a little lonesome.

And I think the whole sharable economy idea is really taking off, particularly for young people. The internet has strengthened that possibility, with car sharing, Airbnb, and things like that. But what I love about Little Free Libraries

is that they're old school. Sharing isn't just a subset of what the internet can do.

Little Free Libraries are also happening at a time when e-readers and e-books are taking off. They're happening at a time when Amazon has shrunk the number of bookstores. Everybody loves a bookstore, but there are fewer of them. Little Free Libraries, in a sense, spread the pleasure of browsing. It's easy to go online, find exactly the book you want, and it'll be at your house in two days, but you don't get the opportunity to browse. Little Free Libraries are an oasis of serendipity in what is a fairly programmed age.

Most people install Little Free Libraries in their front yards, next to a sidewalk, if possible. But others are installed in public parks, in hospitals, or at schools. Where do you think the Little Libraries can do the most good? Or where would you like more to spring up?

They could do a lot of good in lower-income neighborhoods. Business districts could be good places for them, encouraging people to linger. Parks could be good places for them—because some parks can have a pretty empty, lonesome feeling—especially large parks that are essentially just playing fields.

I think part of the mission of our society, if we want to reconnect community, is just to get people to physically gather together more often. And I think a Little Free Library is just one more reason to pop over to the coffee shop; one more reason to head over to the park; one more reason to go downtown or go to the neighborhood business district or go to the next block. I think overall it's an exciting development that just puts a little more delight into our days.

Grow Literacy

USING LITTLE FREE LIBRARIES TO CELEBRATE READING

*"I do believe
something very magical
can happen when
you read a good book."*

—J. K. ROWLING

CHAPTER 4
GROW LITERACY

For a bibliophile, Little Free Libraries are pocket-size meccas. Where else, other than your bedside table, can you go for books twenty-four hours a day? The Little Libraries put in motion a perpetual book swap of folklore and westerns, first fiction and memoirs, inviting us to dip in for a book adventure we might not have otherwise found. They get neglected books off our dusty shelves and into the hands of delighted readers. And they remind us that for every great book we've read, ten more are waiting—perhaps just down the block.

In short, they are made for people who really, truly love books.

Little Free Libraries also cultivate future bibliophiles. When kids visit a Little Library, they get excited about books, which can translate into a lifetime of reading and all the advantages that brings. A body of research shows that voluminous reading is one of the most important things we can do to ensure academic achievements and a happy, successful life. And according to an international study from the University of Nevada, led by sociologist Mariah Evans, having access to books at home significantly increases a child's level of education. A home library of five hundred books propels a child 3.2 years further in school, on average, but even as few as twenty books—a number that easily fits in a Little Free Library—can make a difference.

At the Peace Project in Laguna de Apoyo, Nicaragua—where increasing literacy is a priority—Little Free Library #6968 provides easy access to books, evening the playing field for underserved children. "In our community, many of the adults are illiterate and/or undereducated," says Michael Ludin, a volunteer with the project. "Finding ways to make reading and education fun and engaging is crucial. If the Little Free Library can encourage one child to enjoy reading, we think it is a success."

This chapter follows a selection of stewards who use their Little Free Libraries to spread the book love.

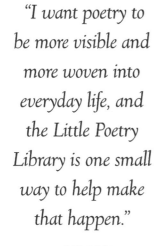

"*I want poetry to be more visible and more woven into everyday life, and the Little Poetry Library is one small way to help make that happen.*"

—CAROLYN
WILLIAMS-NOREN

CAROLYN WILLIAMS-NOREN

Minneapolis, Minnesota, USA

Charter Number: 9398

Poetry is too often kept high on the shelf, like heirloom china you bring out once a year and whisper around so it doesn't break. But poet Carolyn Williams-Noren and her Little Poetry Library are getting poems—delicate or hard bitten—into the daily lives of anyone who strolls by the Blue Moon Coffee Café.

"The Little Poetry Library is a Little Library especially for poetry—books, chapbooks, and periodicals," Williams-Noren explains. "I wanted to create a place in my neighborhood where people can stumble upon poems, and a way for poetry lovers to send poetry out into the world."

Williams-Noren started the Little Library with the help of an Artist Initiative Grant from the Minnesota State Arts Board, which also helped facilitate her written work. She chose to erect the Library outside a popular Longfellow neighborhood coffee shop, where it would get lots of traffic and regular visitors, and launched it with—what else—an energetic and well-attended poetry reading.

"I feel a great sense of satisfaction and connection in the act of creating and tending to a *place,* and making public places for poetry is especially important to me," Williams-Noren says. "As a writer and reader, I know that poetry contains deep vitality—a questioning, an attentiveness—for which we have a great need, as individuals and as a community. I want poetry to be more visible and more woven into everyday life, and the Little Poetry Library is one small way to help make that happen."

The Little Poetry Library was beautifully collaged by RetroFutures Designs' Molly Keenan, a local artist who uses text and images from vintage books in her work, and painted by her partner Aaron Lichtov. It features famous and unknown poets, children and adults, poems and words about poetry, and images that evoke a sense of an urban neighborhood. For Keenan, who grew up as the daughter of Twin Cities poet Deborah Keenan—whose core social group was made up of poets—the commission was very personal and linked to early memories of the poetry and poets in her life.

Keenan and Lichtov live only a block away from Blue Moon and were already fans of the other Little Free Libraries in the neighborhood. "Part of the reason we were so thrilled that Carolyn contacted Molly in August with the invitation to collage the Little Poetry Library is that we had spent that entire summer biking around the neighborhood 'trolling' the many LFLs of Longfellow," Lichtov says. "I would have Ezra (our kid) on a trail-a-bike behind my bike, and Molly would have large panniers on her bike loaded up with a few books culled from our house to donate. As we biked, it became a game to see who would spot the next Little Free Library first."

The Little Poetry Library has become an active part of the neighborhood and a reliable outpost for poetry, with patrons lingering over publications that

appear and disappear regularly, such as Kazim Ali's *The Fortieth Day*, Juliet Patterson's *The Truant Lover*, and the *Mid-American Review*.

A special visitor was poet Éireann Lorsung, author of *Her book*, who spent a month as writer-in-residence at the Little Poetry Library. Invited by Coffee House Press through their CHP in the Stacks library residency program, Lorsung created a book of hours—traditionally, an illuminated book of the Middle Ages; this one, a watercolored devotional to the everyday activity at the Little Library.

"I used books from the Little Poetry Library as points of inspiration alongside plants growing in the neighborhood, people in the café, and the sky I could see through the window," Lorsung says. (Her favorite book to show up? Eleni Sikelianos's *Body Clock*.) "I wanted to engage with people as part of this project; acknowledging the neighborhood and its inhabitants seemed to me to be fundamental," she says. "I enjoyed all the people who stopped to talk with me, but especially the ones who didn't have a predetermined idea about what art or poetry was and who just wanted to talk about their days."

Little Poetry Library steward Williams-Norens hopes the Library will bring positive changes, big or small, to all the community's residents: "I believe that a public, free collection of poetry books is as likely as anything in our neighborhood to provide the insight, connection, and beauty that could change a person's life for the better," she says.

826LA

In the novel and movie *The Book Thief*, Liesel Meminger—a spirited girl growing up in tyrannical Nazi Germany—steals a book (then two, then three), and her life is changed forever by a passion for reading. The writing and tutoring center 826LA hopes the books in its Little Free Library will spark a similar devotion in its students.

A Little Free Library's open access to books—in stark contrast to Liesel's world—inspired *The Book Thief*'s 20th Century Fox film crew to partner with B-Reel production company and build two large-scale Little Free Libraries for 826LA and 826NYC. The Libraries feature miniatures of the German village where Liesel lived and a scene from the film that culminates in a book burning. Tiny singed books lie in the recreated cobblestone street.

"We wanted to tell Liesel's story, allowing kids to share books and get passionate about them in the same way that she is," says Eva Mautino of B-Reel. "The partnership with 826 was the perfect sealing of the idea since they are so locally connected with the community."

826 National was started by author Dave Eggers and educator Nínive Calegari in 2002 in San Francisco; now there are eight total chapters around the country. The sites offer free after-school homework, reading, and writing help for students ages six to eighteen; arts-inspired workshops where kids learn about bookmaking, playwriting, cartooning, and more; plus opportunities to professionally publish their work. Each 826 chapter has a far-out store that sells unusual goods following its theme, from capes, masks, and grappling hooks at the Brooklyn Superhero Supply Co. at 826NYC to a Jungle Hygiene Kit at the Bigfoot Research Institute at 826 Boston.

The Book Thief Library is a fine addition to 826LA's Mar Vista neighborhood site, says 826LA executive director Joel Arquillos. "The design of the Little Library that was installed in front of our shop in Mar Vista looks like it comes from the nineteenth century—which works perfectly with our store in that location, which is a Time Travel Mart from 1882." (Stop by if you need to buy time traveler supplies like Barbarian Repellant or an Evil Robot Memory Eraser.)

The kids who come to 826LA were floored by their new Little Free Library. "They couldn't believe the books were free. That was the thing that they were most blown away by at first," Arquillos says. "Then we told them the idea was they could take one, but if they could also share one, the Library would also help serve others folks in the community."

Since the Little Free Library was installed at 826LA, it has helped strengthen the symbiotic relationship between 826LA and the surrounding community. First, more community members stop by to check out the Library and learn about the 826 organization, which ultimately brings in more volunteer tutors. Even better, the Library serves as a place to showcase students' writing: 826LA publishes fifteen or more chapbooks of student work each year—including titles like *Crazy Is a Seahorse Shadow*, *A Better Universe than the Real Universe*, and *A Fireplace with Cold Fire in It*—and now, copies are available in the Little Free Library for visitors to take and read.

JOCELYN HALE

Minneapolis, Minnesota, USA

Charter Number: 1505

A Little Free Library is no place for book snobbery, finds Jocelyn Hale, executive director of the Loft Literary Center, one of the nation's leading literary arts venues. Instead of culling the less-than-scholarly literature from her Library, Hale learns to appreciate the highbrow and lowbrow, embracing a wider book-loving democracy.

" It was love at first sight. My eye caught an elegant little structure across the lane in a village of England's Cotswolds region. I called to my husband, "Glenn! Look at this . . . a little free library. What a great idea." Not knowing that we had stumbled onto an international community-building movement, we chalked it up to the region's cultural charm. After all, this part of the world brought us Jane Austen and Beatrix Potter. The misting rain enticed my husband and me to linger under the eave that protected the Little Free Library. We studied the books and took one about the history of Stonehenge, a perfect gift because we were visiting the ancient site the next morning.

A few days later, we left the book at an exchange in a local coffee shop. I've always been thrilled by sharing bookshelves when traveling. As a book lover,

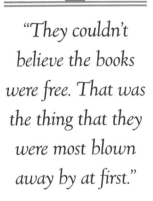

"They couldn't believe the books were free. That was the thing that they were most blown away by at first."

—JOEL ARQUILLOS

checking out the free exchanges is like opening a box in your grandmother's attic—will you find treasures or uninteresting junk? Once, in Guatemala, I had run out of books in English and was compelled to read a series of paperback Louis L'Amour adventures I found at a youth hostel. As I turned page after page into the night, I realized the dark side of literary snobbery—I was missing some really entertaining books. By adding diversity into my reading, my passion for literature deepened.

Soon after my first encounter with the British Little Free Library, I started seeing the oversized birdhouses offering books in my own neighborhood. Walking the dog became a bibliophile's dream. When I spot a Little Free Library down the street, I first admire the creativity of the exterior decorating. I've seen red barns, country cottages, modernist collages, and elegant manor houses. When I reach my destination, I open the door and peruse the collection. I study the offerings—is this a highly curated book experience or more of a communal mishmash? I've started to shape my walking route to pass the Little Free Libraries that match my reading taste.

Many book lovers secretly dream of working in a small bookstore so we can spend our days creating community around books—talking about them, sharing

MARGRET ALDRICH

them, helping others connect with the perfect selection. In a way, participating in a Little Free Library gives you the chance to have your own bookstore experience with the advantage of knowing right from the beginning that this is not a moneymaking operation.

After admiring Little Free Libraries for a year, Glenn and I finally installed our own (painted forest green). We felt like mini-Carnegie spawn. We live on a busy street, so our Little Free Library gets a lot of traffic. I admit, we've been through an evolution with our oversight. I call it the three stages of Little Free Libraries.

My husband and I are both book nuts with literally hundreds (thousands?) of books in our house. They've outgrown our bookshelves and lay piled along the walls in several rooms. At first, our Little Free Library was a way to weed our collection with the added joy of passing along some wonderful reading material. The quality of books was high, and the turnover was swift. This was the dawn of our Little Free Library stewardship. We'd peek out the window and delight in seeing people loiter and then take a book. We considered posting notes with staff recommendations and hosting author readings.

Soon though, we had to face our demons. Our Little Free Library was doing just what it should and moved beyond our offerings into a communal exchange. Bodice-popping romances, marriage and fad diet advice, and dogmatic religious books were nestled together with literary classics and critically acclaimed books from independent nonprofit presses. We'd sneak out to our Little Free Library at night and extricate the offenders. Then I realized we were banning books! What was next, book burning? We had become the enemy.

The very essence of the Little Free Library philosophy is to promote a book-loving democracy—to create a place where neighbors can share literature (in its broadest definition) in an open and adventurous spirit. I love the Little Free Libraries' currency in print books. I have nothing against e-books, but I'd rather hold a paper volume in my hands. Little Free Libraries only deal with the remnants of the physical manifestation of our books. There is a power in exchanging an object rather than an electronic file. Once, I realized I had two copies of a spectacular oversized art book and rather than sell it, I offered it as a gift to an anonymous passerby. The book sat in the Little Free Library next to a sci-fi paperback thriller, and they both disappeared within the hour. **"**

CURATING YOUR COLLECTION

Most Little Free Libraries end up with a delightful hodgepodge of books inside—and that's part of their charm. But you can also thoughtfully choose books for your Library, whether for a particular audience, genre, or time of year.

Play favorites
When you first launch your Library, stock it with your top twenty favorite books of all time. Think back to different times in your life and the books that meant the most to you, challenged you, or changed you. This is a surefire way to show your personality (what says more about a person than what they like to read?) and share some great books with your community.

Pick a theme
Give your Library a narrow focus by choosing one subject that you're passionate about and stocking it with only those books.

Double-decker
If your Library has more than one shelf, designate one for adult books and one for children's books to make it easier for visitors to find the perfect title for them. Or, you can use a divider to separate books for grownups and kids.

Month by month
Look up what "national month" it is—Black History Month, National Poetry Month, or National Pet Month, for example—and stock your Library accordingly, with one book from that subject area or a dozen. Include a note in your Library that explains what month you're recognizing.

Pay attention
Do all of your kids' books instantly fly off the shelves? Or is it adult fiction that disappears most quickly? Once you get to know what your patrons are most apt to pick up, try to keep that genre stocked.

On holiday

Follow the calendar with your Little Free Library inventory. Add a few self-improvement titles around New Year's resolution time, love poems at Valentine's Day, war stories over Memorial Day weekend, novels of personal or political independence on the Fourth of July, gothic horror at Halloween, and beautifully illustrated children's books at Hanukkah, Christmas, and Kwanzaa.

EVGENIA PIROG

Kyiv, Ukraine

Charter Numbers: 7331, 7332, 7340, and others

There are 104 Little Free Libraries in Ukraine, all inspired by Evgenia Pirog's first LFL in Kyiv. Inside and out, the Libraries are geared to nurture kids' inner artists: They are brightly decorated with robots and cakes, lions and poppies—often painted by the children themselves. And they hold fantastical anthologies of stories, poems, and artworks, also created by the local kids who visit.

What is the story of your Little Free Libraries? Why did you decide to build them, and what makes them special?

In the spring of 2012, I started to make these special shelves with free books for children to read. As a writer and mother, I really wanted children to read more, especially printed books. My birdhouse-style Little Free Library immediately got children's interest. And adults', of course. I had many friends—librarians, writers, teachers, artists, students, and parents—who wanted to make birdhouses for books in different cities. Within a year, we made 104 birdhouses in five cities in Ukraine.

The project became a countrywide initiative called Add Reading, where everyone can "add" books, friends, reading, knowledge, emotions, and talent. My dream of creating a reading environment for children came true.

What books are in your Little Free Library right now?

There is a unique collection of books in our Libraries: almanacs of tales that children create with writers. There are already twelve of these anthologies of children's art. Sergey Grydin, a modern children's writer, actively engages children in this creative activity. We dream that children in many countries will create such anthologies. We all can share and better understand the world.

Books and magazines for children are also found in most of our free Libraries, as well as educational publications and books for adults. Adults reading books are perfect examples for children, aren't they? Writers and publishers of children's books support our project, too. Together we are opening the world of books to children.

How do you make the kid-created anthologies?

We invite groups of children (four to thirty persons, age four to fourteen years) and artists (one to three persons). Then we discuss the topic and coinvent the story. Children draw the characters and illustration elements. Usually this creative improvisation lasts one hour. During the meeting, the writer edits the text, and the designer makes the layout artwork.

All participants feel fantastic emotion. Children associate it with books and reading. This is wonderful! My great *Silver Book* was recognized as a national record holder in the *Holos Ukrayiny* newspaper: 360 children and 60 adults created it.

How are your Little Free Libraries designed and decorated?

Each of our Little Free Libraries has a unique design. A young sixteen-year-old artist, Stas Melnychuk, painted space robots with books on one. Another Little Free Library in a children's café has an ornament of chocolates and sweets.

In Lviv, a Little Library in Children's Art School is decorated with paper flowers. Four classes of elementary school students together painted the Library and take care of the books. Now the children read more.

How have the libraries had an impact on your community?

The idea of giving children more books and opportunities brought together many people and organizations. Libraries, the Department of Education, and community youth organizations all joined the project in Rivne. A librarian and writer, Irene Matsko, brought together colleagues, patrons, students, and school authorities in Ternopil. Artists, educators, writers, librarians, and singers got creative with the children and me for the Add Reading initiative in Kyiv. Others have started artistic projects to popularize reading among children. Working together makes people more tolerant and makes a more stable community.

"As a writer and mother, I really wanted children to read more, especially printed books."

—EVGENIA PIROG

NANCY VOGL AND DAVID STRANGE

Traverse City, Michigan, USA

Charter Number: 6315

This sunny Little Free Library was made for Traverse City, Michigan's smallest citizens: kids. Painted an inviting yellow, stocked with only children's books, and located a stone's throw from a local ice cream shop, the Cherry Tree Children's Library catches the attention of every child who walks by.

With books and building in their blood, Nancy Vogl and David Strange are ideal stewards: Vogl is the author of the award-winning children's book *Am I a Color Too?*, while Strange has more than thirty-five years' experience building all kinds of structures, including geodesic dome homes in northern Michigan. After Vogl happened upon a Little Library while on a walk, she cajoled her able husband into helping her build one.

"We built our Little Free Library, specifically for children only, as a way to reinforce the importance of reading," Vogl says. "We see way too many young people with their heads down looking at electronic devices, and we don't want them to lose the magic of holding a book in their hands. We have ten adult children and thirteen grandchildren (and counting!), and even the adult children are too immersed in technology. We see physical books as a way to reinforce creativity, with the touch and feel of books as reminders of connecting on more of a human level."

The charming yellow house—trimmed with colorful shutters and tidy flower boxes—was inspired by the architecture of Traverse City but introduces a whimsical quality that draws young visitors. It was built almost entirely with reclaimed wood and other materials, Vogl says, and took two months to construct. With the exception of the little door and octagon window on the front and the staircase and railing inside, she and Strange created every aspect

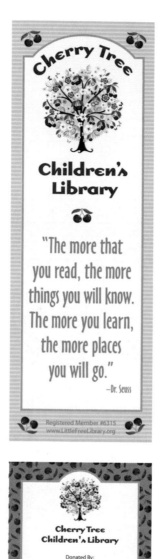

of the Cherry Tree Children's Library: Strange built the structure to scale, fashioning each piece of siding, each window, the shutters, flower boxes, and more. Vogl did the painting and decorating, and created the stone chimney from rocks she collected from the beach on Lake Michigan. She also made the miniature books held by the figures of children inside the Library.

The Little Library even holds a few surprises. There are "secret" doors for children to discover and open. The bottom one houses a bookmark with a quote from Dr. Seuss that says, "The more that you read, the more things you will know. The more you learn, the more places you will go." Open the upper door, and you'll find a little girl reading *Clifford, the Big Red Dog*, as well as tiny cards for children to take home, with affirmations to reinforce reading and self-esteem.

Vogl, who counts *Anne of Green Gables* as her favorite childhood book, is thrilled to share a love of reading with so many of the kids in her community. "Cherry Tree Children's Library is located one block from the Grand Traverse West Bay, across the street from one of the busiest tourist eateries in town and just a half block away from a super-busy seasonal ice cream shop," she says. "Because of its location, lots of neighbors and tourists are enjoying sitting on the white bench opposite the Library, where they can read to their children, and kids enjoy sitting in one of the small red Adirondack chairs next to the Library."

"We're constantly seeing people taking pictures, and the best reactions have been from the adults. It's as if our Little Library is reminding them of their childhood," she continues. "We get e-mails and phone calls, too—people in the neighborhood thanking us for doing something so meaningful for the children. We receive great joy watching the reactions of people, knowing we didn't just put a up a Library; we created an experience."

Their Little Free Library is maintained as a lending library—not a traditional LFL where patrons can keep the books they find—so Vogl and Strange include a boilerplate inside each book that states the books are to be returned. Sometimes they're returned with a bonus: "A book from one of my publishers is *Little Yellow Pear Tomatoes*," Vogl explains. "Someone had borrowed it, and when they returned the book, it was placed face front with a little package of yellow pear tomatoes next to it. What a surprise!"

The Cherry Tree Children's Library has given countless rewards to its stewards and to the kids of Traverse City. And Vogl is delighted that it also reinforces the importance of reading in the community. "Little Free Libraries are important because they are a visible reminder of the value and beauty found in reading. As our Library is located on a busy street, one of the main entrances into the neighborhood, it's a daily reminder for hundreds of people that books are alive and well."

MARGRET ALDRICH

TYPE RIDER II: THE TANDEM POETRY TOUR

Boulder, Colorado, to Beloit, Wisconsin, USA

Charter numbers: Multiple

Last July, Amy Tingle and Maya Stein embarked on a big adventure: in a single month, they rode a tandem bike more than a thousand miles from Colorado to Wisconsin, building Little Free Libraries and writing crowdsourced poetry along the way.

The women established a total of twenty-five Little Free Libraries on their journey, in small towns like Brady, Nebraska; Indianola, Iowa; and Greeley, Colorado. The Amish Shed–style Libraries were donated to the towns free of charge and built in public parks, at coffee shops, on bike trails, and in yards. Often entire neighborhoods would come out to help. "It was really fun to see how communities got together to build these, and the artwork on some of them was just wonderful," Stein says.

In addition to Little Free Libraries, Stein and Tingle brought poetry to the towns. Throughout the trip, they offered a "tandem poetry" activity as part of the Little Free Libraries' grand opening events. During the activity, a resident would give them a word or short phrase, and the women would each write a

poem, side by side on their typewriters. Some of the words they were given included *cottonwood, unicorn, old cowboys,* and *schadenfreude.*

Stein and Tingle, who teach art and creative writing classes in their home state of New Jersey and beyond, created the tandem poetry activity, in part, to show that writing is accessible to everyone. "We think that too often, people feel a sense of mystery and elusiveness around writing or art, which perhaps prevents them from trying something new creatively, because they somehow don't feel 'qualified,'" Stein says.

As they typed out each poem, they hoped the recipients might be

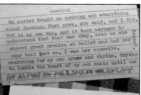

inspired to challenge themselves creatively. "What we never really expected was the intimacy of the exchange. How powerful it was to write poems specifically for someone else. And the quiet energy that hummed between us as all the poems came into view," Stein says. "We also felt it was important to read the poems aloud to the person who gave us their word or phrase. It was an additional way to connect, but also it helped each of us to become stronger writers by listening to the poems the other wrote. We both found the experience enriching in so many ways."

The small-town vibe agreed with the couple—who have a Little Free Library in their own front yard—and wherever the decade-old Cannondale bike took them, they were warmly greeted. "We felt such a sense of welcome," Stein says. "We live in a very busy and dense part of the country—just twelve miles west of Manhattan—and we see how the proximity of neighbors makes everybody very possessive of their privacy. So we were pleasantly surprised by how the people we met during our travels in July were so enthusiastic about connecting. It was lovely to experience, and something of that positivity surely rubbed off on us."

BOOKS AROUND THE BLOCK

Minneapolis, Minnesota, USA

Charter Number: Multiple

One hundred Little Free Libraries are coming to underserved areas of the City of Lakes. Through a program called Books around the Block, Little Free Library and Minneapolis Public Schools (MPS) are collaborating to bring a Little Library to every block in North Minneapolis, one of the most impoverished districts of the city.

Through the program—which was dreamed up by Todd Bol and Melanie Sanco, director of the resource development and innovation department at MPS—Minneapolis families and school sites can apply to become Little Free Library stewards, at no cost to them. Books around the Block helps with everything from construction to installation to book sourcing, making the project accessible to households of any income level.

"Parents who have books in the home increase the level of education their children will attain up to two grade levels, regardless of economic status or education level of parents," says Olivia Quintanilla, the Books around the Block

> "Parents who have books in the home increase the level of education their children will attain up to two grade levels."
>
> —OLIVIA QUINTANILLA

MARGRET ALDRICH

project lead for MPS. "We also know that 61 percent of homes living in poverty do not have age-appropriate books in the home. Nearly 90 percent of MPS students living in North Minneapolis live in poverty."

The hope is that by having Little Free Libraries on every block, books are more likely to filter into kids' and adults' everyday routines. "Instead of finding books only in schools or public libraries, Books around the Block allows kids and adults to find things to read on their daily walk, and take books home with them," Quintanilla says. "Being able to find good books at different grade levels will help attract new readers. It can also encourage parents to improve their own reading skills. Access to free books will help build home libraries, encourage reading, and build a community that shares and rejoices in books."

Books around the Block is a national effort, serving other parts of the country as well. Community organizers, school liaisons, teachers, and individuals can contact Little Free Library to receive a program guide and hear how their neighborhoods can benefit.

DECATUR BOOK FESTIVAL

Decatur, Georgia, USA

Charter Number: Multiple

"*Seeing someone read a book you love is like seeing a book recommend a person.*"

The historic town of Decatur, Georgia—six miles east of Atlanta and just four square miles in size—hosts the country's biggest independent book festival. Held in the town's walkable downtown square, the Decatur Book Festival (DBF) draws thousands of book lovers every August to celebrate all things literary with author panels, book signings, poetry slams, and children's activities, as well as music performances, food, beer, and wine. At one of their most recent festivals, DBF organizers included Little Free Libraries in the lineup.

Twelve Little Libraries were built by Michael Montgomery, painted by Atlanta-area artists, and put up for auction as an event fundraiser. Featured artists included editorial cartoonist Mike Luckovich (black-and-white LFL), children's book author and illustrator Elizabeth Dulemba (fairy LFL), *Pete the Cat* illustrator James Dean (Pete the Cat LFL), and contemporary painter Ruth Franklin (Penguin Books LFL). "The auction was a huge success," says festival executive director Darren Wang, with Libraries fetching seven hundred dollars and more.

MARGRET ALDRICH

"In many ways, we see the Little Free Libraries as the embodiment of the spirit of the Decatur Book Festival. The sense of community is certainly central to it, but also the conversations that come out of them," says Wang. "There's a quote that's been making the rounds lately—'Seeing someone read a book you love is like seeing a book recommend a person.' People love to talk about the stories they love, and the Little Libraries make that possible."

LISA LOPEZ

El Paso, Texas, USA

Charter Number: 239 and others

What do you do when your city is ranked one of the least literate places in the country? El Paso, Texas, is the fourth least literate city in the United States and falls dead last for number of bookstores per capita. When a school librarian named Lisa Lopez brought a Little Free Library to the city's Zavala Elementary School, however, kids started to get excited about reading. It was the first Little Library in Texas—and the first time one had been placed inside a school.

Lopez was born in El Paso, but grew up just across the border in Ciudad Juarez, Chihuahua, Mexico, where books were scarce. After returning to El Paso as a teenager, the first thing she did was get a library card. Lopez eventually earned a Master of Library and Information Science degree at the University of North Texas and made it her mission to improve the literary outlook of her borderland city, going on to win *Library Journal*'s Movers and Shakers award. Fifty Little Free Libraries later, the bilingual librarian doesn't show signs of stopping.

Why did you decide to bring Little Free Libraries to El Paso?

The main reasons why I decided to take on the Little Free Library craze were because our students were no longer going to receive free reading materials from Reading is Fundamental, since the Federal budget slashed the monies for that, and because El Paso has been rated one of the most illiterate cities in the nation. I decided to reach out to the Little Free Library founders, and they believed in me to such degree that they named me the El Paso Little Free Library Ambassador. My goal to spread these free book exchanges across the borderland became a reality in late 2011, and we are still going strong with more than fifty Little Libraries citywide.

MARGRET ALDRICH

The very first Little Free Library in El Paso was installed inside the Zavala Elementary library. I had a group of stellar fourth- and fifth-grade students paint it and take care of it. In other words, they became the stewards. I also allowed exemplary students to autograph it with glitter pens. This indoor Little Library became the talk of the school. Students were bringing tons of books from home and exchanging them for new ones. Even parents were bringing boxes full of old books. A couple of weeks later, Todd Bol donated an authentic Amish-made barn look-alike Little Free Library to Zavala. The entire school community was mesmerized with the new outdoor Library.

As Mr. Bol and I continued to collaborate in coming up with ideas to spread Little Free Libraries across the borderland, he decided to mention us in *USA Today*'s article on LFLs, which spread the word of our efforts as a campus and city to improve literacy rates, advocate for Libraries, and enhance a sense of community, sharing, and recycling. We became popular with news and media groups, which led to a long and enjoyable journey of spreading Little Free Libraries with the help of local library associations, educational institutions, businesses, city departments, and dedicated woodworkers.

What meaningful interactions have happened because of your Little Free Libraries?

The very first publication on our Zavala Little Free Library came from the *El Paso Times,* which contained a wonderful article on our efforts as a campus to spread a love of reading. Within a couple of days from this being published, I received several packages and boxes filled with children's books. They came from Sugarland and Houston, Texas, from a group of retired teachers who came across our *El Paso Times* article. They kept donating and donating a myriad of wonderful kid's books over the course of one year. Students were eager to see what books were being donated every time they saw a library package or box. It warmed our hearts knowing that our efforts were being applauded from far away and nearby.

How were your Little Free Libraries designed and decorated?

The school Little Free Libraries tend to have a lot of colors to attract the student populations. It is essential to allow the community to have a say in the design and paint job of their Little Library. This is to enhance that sense of ownership and thus better stewardship. At Zavala Elementary, I actually held an LFL design contest. The winner received a mini Little Free Library (which Todd Bol kindly donated), second place got a gingerbread house, and third prizewinner got a small wooden birdhouse.

How have your Libraries had an impact on your community?

The Little Free Library phenomenon has impacted our border region in such a way that excitement for literacy is multiplying at an unprecedented rate. Ranked as the fourth least literate city in the nation, the city of El Paso has embraced this grassroots literacy movement! The city's Parks and Recreation Department, alongside the Department of Public Health, adopted the initiative by allowing these free book exchanges to be installed at their facilities. So far, a total of fifteen WIC (Women, Infant, and Children) clinics requested Little Libraries. In addition, two city parks have requested them for their park visitors to enjoy. Another twenty-five El Paso Independent School District campuses established Little Free Libraries at their school sites. Lastly, several nonprofit agencies—such as the Child Crisis Center, Center Against Family Violence, and Project Vida—also installed Little Free Libraries at their centers, where so many individuals and families get help.

MARGRET ALDRICH

Do you have advice for other Little Free Library stewards?

In my humble opinion, children make the best stewards. They just love being made caretakers of something they take pride in. I noticed how they thoroughly enjoy the publicity and viewing how the free book exchanges are doing globally. My students were so proud to have the first Little Free Library in the state of Texas, the first Little Free Library in El Paso, and first school anywhere to install a Little Free Library.

CELEBRATE BOOKS

Little Free Libraries attract both lifelong book lovers and fledgling readers. Make the written word something for everyone to enjoy with these ideas for bookish revelry.

■ Invite your Little Free Library patrons—adults and kids—to add their own written works to the Library. Short stories, homemade comic books, and poems of all kinds can be added to a communal binder in the Library that can be "checked out" and returned. Novelists can include works-in-progress and get feedback from friendly neighborhood critics. Any local authors can donate books they've written and published.

■ Start a book club in your neighborhood. To get people involved, invite participants through word of mouth and by posting a notice in your Little Free Library. Make the book choice a democratic process: List four possible book selections in a notebook in your Library, along with paper ballots and a box where people can cast their vote. Set a meeting time and place, gather to discuss the book and get to know each other, and at the end of the meeting, encourage members to donate that month's book to local Little Free Libraries.

■ Arrange the books in your Little Free Library to create spine poetry. Here's how it works: Imagine that a book title, which appears on the

MARGRET ALDRICH

book's spine, is one line of poetry. Stack books so the spines create a poem. (Looking at my bookshelf, I can find this poem in the book spines, for example: *Let the dark flower blossom / before night falls. / Time for outrage, / atonement, / her.*) Post a note in your Library asking visitors to create their own spine poems and record them in a notebook.

Let the Dark Flower Blossom
Before Night Falls
Time for Outrage
Atonement
Her

■ Host storytime at your Little Free Library. Find out what inspires the children in your neighborhood—from giant squid to Pokemon to fashion design— and select books in those subject areas. Take turns reading aloud to each other then discuss what you've read. What did the kids learn from the book? What did they want to know more about? Have them draw an alternate book cover. If the book is fiction, have them write an alternate ending.

Be Creative

USING LITTLE FREE LIBRARIES TO KICKSTART CREATIVITY

"Books have
a life
of their own."

—LATIN PROVERB

CHAPTER 5
BE CREATIVE

Like snowflakes, poems, and people, Little Free Libraries are fantastically diverse. Each one is unique in some way, from the design to the materials, the paint job to the accoutrements. Even standard Little Free Libraries—such as the Two-Story Brownstone or Cedar Roof Basic, bought from the organization itself—are often embellished by stewards with a favorite literary quote, a small mural, or a subtle detail before they unveil them to the neighborhood.

Chicago art history professor Delia Cosentino was drawn to the Little Free Library concept, in part, because it gave her a chance to flex her creative muscles. "Since I'm not crafty with wood, I decided to buy the structure and personalize it," she says. "The back of the roof features a rendition of Van Gogh's *Starry Night,* while the front highlights a kind of modernist sun in bright colors across a black sky. The idea is that the sun is rising over its front door—a sign of the enlightenment within."

This opportunity for creativity and self-expression is one of the coolest things about Little Free Libraries. They stand as small examples of street art, characteristic of the individuals who made them, allowing stewards to communicate their personalities and celebrate their cultures—or just make something colorful, quirky, and memorable.

JOHN AND DOROTHY SWEET

Bend, Oregon, USA

Charter Number: 4411

Looking for artist John Sweet of Bike Gate Studio? Check the nearest flea market, bicycle shop, garage sale, discount warehouse, or thrift store. Sweet is inspired by found or unconventional materials and often incorporates them into his fused-glass art pieces. When he decided to build a Little Free Library, he was sure it would incorporate a mélange of repurposed objects.

"I knew that I wanted to use one of the aluminum library road signs for the roof," Sweet says, "and a search on eBay turned one up that had outlived its useful life." The other pieces of the Library turned up one by one: "The wood came from a remodel project in our dining room. I found a metal picture frame at a garage sale that worked as a doorframe. Some recycled bike gears and a couple of old pieces of copper that I had picked up at Pak It Liquidators were transformed into a vase of fused-glass flowers for one side. A stylized 'Bend Cruiser' became the fused-glass piece I created for the door. And a box of kids' maple building blocks, picked up at a garage sale, added texture to the post."

The mishmash of materials resulted in a quietly sophisticated Little Free Library that attracts visitors daily. "John Sweet's Library is an awesome artistic achievement," says Nate Pedersen, a librarian at the Deschutes Public Library in Bend. "It demonstrates the extraordinary room for human creativity that can go into making a Little Free Library."

EOWYN AND JESSE SAVELA

Bellingham, Washington, USA

Charter Number: 11105

"Yarn bombing" is a form of street art in which a public object is wrapped in knit, crochet, or other yarn craft. If you're a knitter with a Little Free Library, you have an opportunity for an art installation right in your own front yard.

The James Street Library stays warm all year long with its chevron sweater, hand-knit by Eowyn Savela and lavished with the attention of her sons Harald and Theodore. Learn how to yarn bomb your Library by following the tutorial on page 247.

MARGRET ALDRICH

MARGRET ALDRICH

What is your Little Free Library's story? Why did you decide to build it, and how did you get started?

Little Free Libraries combine so many wonderful things, it's hard to keep track of them all: books, sharing books, encouraging reading and literacy, building community, recycling, trying new things, being vulnerable, trust, woodworking, creative problem solving, and really cool yard art, to name a few.

It took me a few months to gather my nerve to give building one a go. My husband and I combined have middle school shop class–level carpentry skills, so the thought of building a Little Free Library was intimidating. But we had a lot of scrap wood that came with our house when we bought it, a great building materials recycler in town, lots of ideas from seeing other Little Free Libraries online, and helpful friends and family. I started with an old kitchen cabinet from the RE Store and went from there. In about a month of working on the weekends, the James Street Library was ready to go.

How is your Little Free Library decorated? Any tips?

I love to knit, and knew from the start that I would yarn bomb our Library. I used yarn I already had, and some from Goodwill, to make a crazy, zigzag, cozy, colorful Library sweater that even has a knitted-in sign saying, "James Street Library."

Besides the yarn bomb, the Library has a gnome/woodsy theme. There is a toadstool knob on the door, and two gnomes who watch over our Library. Frederick the Gnome reads a book underneath and Henrietta the gnome knits away, clipped to the sweater on the side. Toadstool seats were recently added beside the Library.

What meaningful, surprising, or bizarre interactions have happened because of your Little Free Library?

We live on a busy street, right across from an elementary school. One morning, when the Library was quite new, I peeked out the window to find two little girls at the Library. They were on their way to school and had their backpacks unzipped, ready to fill with books, I assumed. It was so heartwarming to see them checking out the Library, and as I watched them, I imagined how thrilled they must be to have discovered this magic box of books.

Later in the day, I checked the Library to see which books they had chosen. I was surprised and proud to find they had left a book instead of taking any. That totally made my day.

"I love to knit, and knew from the start that I would yarn bomb our Library."

—EOWYN SAVELA

A COLLECTION ON DISPLAY

A kaleidoscope of buttons makes Karri Folks's Little Free Library #7082 a vibrant addition to her Ames, Iowa, neighborhood.

"The rooftop is composed of a rainbow of buttons, and each side of the Library has a different motif," she says. "The left side consists of a mosaic of buttons designed to look like a sunny day in a field of flowers; the right side is a mosaic designed as a starry night surrounded by apple and orange trees. The backside of the Library is a colorful rainbow with the message, 'READ!'"

This LFL is a great example of how a personal collection can become the theme of your Library. Folks had collected buttons for years, so they became a natural source for decorating her Library. Other collections that could be put to use include coins, bottle caps (see page 67), Lego pieces, stamps or baseball cards (placed behind the plexiglass), 45 rpm records, rocks, beer cans (cut and flattened), or seashells.

Visitors to your Library may even help feed your collection. "Apparently lots of people here in Iowa have an appreciation for buttons. In fact, some of my visitors have left buttons to share," Folks says.

MARIA OLSEN AND KIRK BRUST

Bloomington, Minnesota, USA

Charter Number: 4048

Whovians will recognize this bright blue police box: it was designed to mimic the TARDIS, the time-traveling vessel from the cult BBC television show *Doctor Who*. By using an iconic object as inspiration for their Little Free Library, the stewards tapped into a built-in fan club, and the Library has drawn visitors from all over the country.

What is your Little Free Library's story? Why did you decide to build it, and what makes it special?

We love to read and always like to share books with friends and family. When we heard about the Little Free Library movement, we knew this would be a great project to participate in. We really like the BBC show *Doctor Who,* and we thought, what better vehicle for a Little Library than the TARDIS? The TARDIS is bigger on the inside, as are books.

What meaningful, funny, or bizarre interactions have happened because of your Little Free Library?

We have a guest book inside that people have left many fantastic comments in. We've had people from Canada, California, Maine, Virginia, Florida, the Dakotas, and more sign in. We just received a request for a couple to take their engagement pictures at the TARDIS LFL—they're having a *Doctor Who*–themed wedding.

And the University of Minnesota *Doctor Who* club—the Gallifreyan Human Alliance—stopped by one rainy, cold Saturday this spring to visit. There were about ten of them. When I went out to say hi, one of them ran up and gave me a big hug. It was fun meeting them and helping them take pictures. They brought books to share and had a great time in spite of the rain.

It has certainly been a neighborhood hit. Even if visitors don't know the *Doctor Who* angle, they are thrilled to find out there are books inside that are free and available to share.

How was your Little Free Library designed and decorated? Any tips?

Kirk Brust, a talented model builder and artist, designed and built the structure from scratch. He studied pictures online and watched *Doctor Who* for inspiration. He made it weather tight and very durable to last through the snowy, cold

winters and the summer weather of sun, wind, rain, and hail. He used cedar wood for its durability and the best primer and paint we could find.

The interior shelves are decorated with old dictionary pages from a 1979 *Webster's Deluxe Unabridged Dictionary* that had great illustrations with many of the definitions. I also put in some old-time animal vignettes to add a splash of color and whimsy. I applied the pages to the painted shelves using Golden Artist Acrylics Regular Gel Medium. This is a great adhesive that also has some UV protection in it. It's a sticky process but gives you a great, durable look.

A later addition to our LFL was a bench. We noticed that some families would sit on the curb and read a story or two, so we decided to add a better place to sit down.

What is the weirdest book (or other item) that has shown up in your Little Free Library?

This is weird but wonderful. A family that visited our Little Free Library, who were avid readers as well as *Doctor Who* fans, left us a very special guest book. They had purchased this at the Doctor Who Experience in Cardiff, Wales, and delivered it to our Library.

They signed the book as follows: "Hello Whovians and Fellow Avid Readers. This guest book was purchased at the Doctor Who Experience in Cardiff, Wales on Monday June 17, 2013, expressly for this little free library. We're pleased to offer a gift of a TARDIS for your TARDIS. The Knutson Family." We were quite taken by this gesture of thoughtfulness.

SUE AND JAIMIE HALLIDAY

San Diego, California, USA

Charter Number: 7739

Sunny San Diego is the perfect home for this Volkswagen bus Library, which reflects the personalities of its VW-loving owners.

"I'm a VW nut," says Sue, who learned to drive in a Beetle and grew up in the beach community of Santa Monica, where VW buses and Beetles were everywhere. Recently the couple even rented a vintage Volkswagen bus for a one-week trip. They had a blast, but with no heat, no air-conditioning, and not enough horsepower, the adventure got the idea of buying one out of their systems. They opted for a VW Library instead.

"I read about the Little Free Library project in the *Los Angeles Times,* and loved the idea," Sue says. "When I mentioned to my husband that I'd found a new project, he knew I'd actually found *him* a new project, but he warmed up to the idea when I told him that once he built and installed it, I'd maintain it." Over the years, Sue's friends had given her model VW buses and a Lego VW bus, so Jaimie used those as models for their Little Library. "Originally it was going to be stained wood, but I really wanted it to be more colorful and eye-catching. We also had glass in the windows but quickly realized that if we wanted to attract kids and minimize risk, plastic would be a better option."

Use the surfboard on top to open the lid and see what's inside—from *Shutter Island* for grownups to *Go, Dog, Go* for kids. "We're in a neighborhood that's shifting from original owners who moved into their homes in the seventies and are now elderly, to young parents of elementary school kids," Sue says. "I arbitrarily divided the Library into half adult and half children's books. The more active half is the children's side by far, which is great."

Keeping the books coming—and age appropriate—hasn't been a problem for the Hallidays. Sue had read an article about a Little Free Library steward who found a book called *Porn for Women* in his Library and quickly pulled it—then realized it was just a book of pictures of men doing housework. "I thought that

was hilarious," Sue says. A similar experience happened when she found a book in her Library called *The Sex Lives of Cannibals.* "I promptly yanked it out of the bus. But there was a little sticky note in it that said, 'A gift for the Library. Don't worry, it's not about sex!' I read the book, which was actually very funny (and, in fact, not about sex) and returned it to the Library with the note intact."

Nonetheless, to accommodate all the kids' and young adult books that circulate, Jaimie is thinking about building a "Woody" Little Free Library. The wood-paneled car, popular with surfers and made famous by Beach Boys' lyrics, would be a perfect partner for their VW bus.

PETER HOMAN AND CHRISTINE WASLANDER

Bergen, North Holland, Netherlands

Charter Number: 4944

One of the tenets of Little Free Library is to upcycle used, cast-off materials whenever you can. In North Holland, Peter Homan and Christine Waslander transformed part of an old arcade game—Pinball Champ '82—into a neighborhood Little Library.

The pinball machine was deconstructed and machinery removed, then the top portion was fitted with plexiglass doors and red handles to finish it off. The Little Library has gotten plenty of attention. "The mayoress of our village came to open our Little Free Library, there was a lot of press in local and national newspapers, and a radio team came to do a live interview," Homan says. "We have a lot of new friends and are more or less famous in our village."

Connected to a Dutch reading project called Fringo, which uses a game based on bingo to get school-age kids excited about books, the Little Library is serving its mission to spread literacy and "make reading a party" (Fringo's motto).

The resurrected pinball machine draws a steady stream of enthusiastic—and generous—visitors, who donate many more books than they take, in many languages. "The mayoress even brought a book in Frisian," says Homan.

BILLY COLLINS

Here, former United States poet laureate Billy Collins talks about why he admires Little Free Libraries' ability to put literature in front of us in unexpected ways.

"

It's one thing to pull down from a shelf in your paneled library a morocco-bound copy of Shelley, sit down in your leather chair, and indulge in some quality poetry time. It's another thing to spot a poem on a billboard, read one on a subway, or see a line of a poem being slowly dragged across the sky by a single-engine airplane. I'm all for poetry in public places, poetry released from the confines of the library and the classroom, poetry that enters the mainstream of American life. I've heard of poetry placed in birdbaths, poetry on the backs of plastic hotel keys, and think how easy it is to put a poem on your refrigerator door.

The Little Free Library is a terrific example of placing books—poetry included—within reach of people in the course of their everyday lives. 'Free' is always a good thing, and the project has a nice give-and-take feel to it. Here's hoping we bump into literature when we turn the next corner—before we have time to resist!

"

MARGRET ALDRICH

UNUSUAL BUILDING MATERIALS

Little Free Libraries have been constructed from everything imaginable. When the polar vortex hit the Upper Midwest in 2014, Doug Senalik of Madison, Wisconsin, even built a temporary one out of ice. (A few book donations were made to it, he says, including *30 Delicious Icebox Cookie Recipes*.)

Think about how you can use unconventional materials or objects for your Little Free Library. Does your town have an old phone booth or newspaper dispenser that is no longer in use? Ask if you can turn it into a Library, either on site or on your personal property.

Some of the other materials resourceful stewards have used to create permanent Little Libraries include:

- doghouses
- toolboxes
- kitchen cabinets
- mailboxes
- milk crates
- minifridges/microwaves
- suitcases
- wine barrels
- dollhouses
- hope chests
- tree trunks
- storage benches
- galvanized washtubs
- circuit-breaker boxes
- bread boxes

KATHY AND LORNE ROSS

Muskoka Lakes, Ontario, Canada

Charter Number: 5017

Here's a Little Free Library we'd all like to find on a hike—an Ontario couple achieves the ultimate in creative reuse when they carve a felled ash tree into a Little Free Library.

What is your Little Free Library's story? Why did you decide to build it, and what makes it special?

After seeing an article in the *Toronto Star* about Little Free Libraries, I knew I wanted to build one on my cottage road. I didn't know what form it would take, but with my husband's vision and design abilities, I knew it would be special. When we were cutting down an old tree and discovered it was hollow, we knew it would make a unique Little Free Library.

Our LFL is a three-season Library. It is in a remote location where the neighbors come in the spring and leave in the fall. We are the only ones who live here full time, so in the winter we remove the books, wrap it in burlap, and wait for spring.

What meaningful, funny, or bizarre interactions have happened because of your Little Free Library?

One day a neighbor I hadn't met asked if I was the steward of the Library. She wanted to give me a big hug and thank me for building the Little Free Library. She said, "It's all about the love of reading."

What books are in your Little Free Library right now?

There are two Alice Munro books, *The Love of a Good Woman* and *Hateship, Friendship, Courtship, Loveship, Marriage*. Summer visitors love good mysteries— there is always a selection of John Grisham, David Baldacci, Minette Walters, Kate Atkinson, and Patricia Cornwell. I try to make sure there are lots of children's books, too. *Goodnight Moon* and *The Runaway Bunny* are there currently.

How did you design and build your Little Free Library?

The Little Free Library tree is an ash. It was standing branchless and dead for a number of years when we decided it should come down before it fell down. As it turned out, it was hollow—the perfect kind of tree for a Little Library. We

painted a preservative on the inside and once it was in place, we filled the bottom part with cement so it wouldn't fall on anyone.

Because there were holes in the tree/Library, I decided to put some jewels in the cement that filled the holes. I also found an eye ring for one side and a happy face bead for the base. I thought the youngest kids would enjoy finding the happy face.

How has the Library had an impact on you?

I have read books that I never would have chosen for myself because someone left them in my Little Free Library. For instance, *Escape from Camp 14: One Man's Remarkable Odyssey from North Korea to Freedom in the West* by Blaine Harden educated me and made a great impact on me. The Dave Eggers novel *A Hologram for the King* is another book I likely would not have chosen but thoroughly enjoyed.

KIERAN AND CHRISTINA LEOPOLD

Iowa City, Iowa, USA

Charter Number: 8297

Iowa City is a longtime friend to books: it's a UNESCO City of Literature (a designation awarded by the United Nations), it's home to the renowned Iowa Writers' Workshop, and it provides funding for citizens who want to build Little Free Libraries through its Program for Improving Neighborhoods.

The Little Free Library at 116 Raven Street is one of the city's most recognizable. It's what steward Kieran Leopold calls "Victorian ramshackle," designed to look like an old haunted house, with a steeply pitched mansard-style roof, widow's walk, lightning rods, and miniature ravens perched atop. The clapboard-siding effect was achieved by hot-gluing hundreds of wooden tongue depressors to the Little Library.

"We have a dangling chandelier over the front porch and spooky purple LED interior lighting activated by opening the door," Leopold says. "The shelves and inside of the bookcase are painted with glow-in-the-dark paint. And we have glow-in-the-dark spiders keeping an eye on the books."

Appropriately enough, the Raven Street Library is filled with (mostly) books to scare. There are classics like *Dracula* and *Frankenstein*, anthologies of ghost stories, horror and suspense novels, and a shelf for younger readers with age-appropriate spooky stories and books about bats and bugs.

The Little Library gets especially busy on Halloween, and Leopold installs an inexpensive motion-activated device that moans, "Go away" whenever someone walks by or opens the Library door. "It was great to see some of the kids were as, or more, excited about the books in the Library as they were about the candy on our porch," Leopold says.

The neighborhood is fully supportive of the Little Free Library, making book donations, embracing the theme, and engaging with each other. The county seat's transit bus has even made stops at the Library, so passengers can check it out.

"My new routine when I return to the house from work or from a weekend away is to stop by the Library, check that the battery is still charged, and try to scope out new books, or check for notes in returned books," Leopold says. "It's like a low-tech social media site—one in which all our neighbors participate."

TRACY MUMFORD

Minneapolis, Minnesota, USA

Charter Number: 1955

When Tracy Mumford moved to Minneapolis in 2010, she was happy to discover that she'd stumbled into what she calls "one of the most bookish towns in America." She was quick to jump into the creative scene, finding work at a small publisher and erecting her own Little Free Library. Her curious tale involves a decapitated mannequin covered in book pages, a penguin named Penny, and an ingenious inter–Little Library loan program.

What is your Little Free Library's story? Why did you decide to build it, and what makes it special?

I saw the Little Free Library website before I ever saw a Little Free Library, and I knew this was the way to unleash my book love on the world. And to clear a little space on my shelves. Luckily my landlord was extremely lenient (it helps that she's my sister) and let me take over a patch in the front yard with my biblioschemes.

While I loved the common dollhouse-esque Libraries, my budget leaned more toward the "junk from the thrift store" option than the "beautifully crafted wood" option. So it was off to the thrift store.

One headless mannequin torso and one vintage bread box later, I had a

Library. I decoupaged the mannequin with old book pages and bolted her to the box. I was pretty sure she'd be stolen or vandalized within her first twenty-four hours, but over a year later, she's still standing. I christened her the Headless Library and kept a blog of Library activity, including a title-by-title list of Library books.

She briefly had company on the front lawn: I built a companion Library for children's books. This one was a penguin lawn ornament bolted to yet another bread box. Sadly, this proved too tempting for vandals, and someone made away with her one winter night. RIP Penny.

What meaningful, surprising, funny, or bizarre interactions have happened because of your Little Free Library?

The headless torso probably catches people's eye more than anything else. But don't forget your signage. In my case, the sign from LFL HQ was not enough. I had to actually tell people, "There are books in here. You should take one," to encourage people. I think they thought it was an overgrown lawn ornament otherwise. There was also some brief confusion with the mailman, who started putting mail in it, but I think we've got it sorted out now.

My favorite stories are just the little ones: the kids next door who come over to read and light up at the picture books in Spanish. The mom who drove her SUV up to the curb, had her kids hop out and all pick up books, and then had them read on the curb for a half an hour.

I initiated an inter–Little Library loan program for a while and sent Minnesota-centric books to Little Free Libraries in other states. I exchanged with Tennessee, Louisiana, and others, and they sent back books that represented their towns.

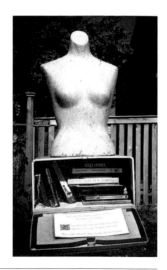

To start my inter–Little Library loan program, I took a look at the LFL map online and picked some other stewards at random from across the country. I dropped them an e-mail with my book-trade scheme, and if they got back to me, we swapped books. The basic idea was to swap books representative of our areas, but sometimes just getting books from their Library was representative enough. People should definitely consider a swap if they're looking to mix up their collections.

What is the weirdest book (or other item) that has shown up in your Little Free Library?

A mushroom-foraging guide, a science book that claimed teachers were lying about dinosaurs in order to further Communism, and a confused grasshopper.

DRAWING ATTENTION

Urban Sketchers Manifesto

•

We draw on location, indoors or out, capturing what we see from direct observation.

•

Our drawings tell the story of our surroundings, the places we live, and where we travel.

•

Our drawings are a record of time and place.

•

We are truthful to the scenes we witness.

•

We use any kind of media and cherish our individual styles.

•

We support each other and draw together.

•

We share our drawings online.

•

We show the world, one drawing at a time.

—URBANSKETCHERS.ORG

Sidewalk cafés, soaring cathedrals, and subway commuters can all be sources of inspiration for Urban Sketchers, an international community whose motto is "Show the World, One Drawing at a Time." From Barcelona to Lisbon, San Francisco to Seoul, sketchers put pen to paper to scratch out images of everyday life, and then share them with other members online.

Capturing Little Free Libraries in her sketchbook allows Renton, Washington, sketcher Mary Katherine Buike to get to know a corner of the city better. "When drawing on location, it slows me down, and I really see the details of the scene," she says. Buike chooses Little Free Libraries as subjects, in part because she likes the culture of sharing and cooperation that they represent.

Anyone with a desire to sketch the world around them can become an urban sketcher; you do not need to be a professional artist. "Silence the self-critic," Buike says. "Draw every day. The more you do it, the more satisfying it becomes. It can be almost meditative." Follow these steps to get started sketching a Little Free Library.

Choose your tools

Do you like to draw in pencil, pen, Sharpie? Are watercolors the medium you like best? What weight of paper do you want to use? Settle on materials that feel good to you and are easy to toss in a bag and carry from location to location.

Find your (little, free) subject

Whether it's a Little Library that you've just discovered, one that you've visited over and over, or the one that stands in your front yard, pick a Little Free Library that speaks to you. Maybe it's interesting because of its design; maybe the location is special; or maybe it's representative of the surrounding neighborhood.

Get to know the Little Free Library

What are its lines, colors, and markings? What does the doorknob look like? What about the roof? Is there any text painted on the Library? Notice the landscape around it, and open the door to see what books are inside.

MARGRET ALDRICH

Pay attention to the surroundings

Notice the people around, especially if the Library is in a public area like a park or business district. What is their posture as they approach the Library? Are they walking with a friend, carrying a to-go coffee cup, chatting on their phone, or bringing a book to donate?

Finish and share

Take your time completing your piece (note that you might want a blanket to sit on, or even a portable folding chair). Once you're finished, share it with friends, your local Urban Sketchers chapter—and the steward of the Library you sketched.

JIM AND DIANE PEIKER,
MISSY AND LOUIE FEHER-PEIKER

Denver, Colorado, USA

Charter Number: 9391

The mansion at the corner of Sixteenth and Race in Denver's Capitol Hill neighborhood was built by architect William Lang in 1889. It featured native lava stone quarried from nearby Castle Rock, an impressive nine-fluted chimney, a four-story tower, and a six-foot example of Impressionist stained glass, popularly known as the Peacock window. Nearly one hundred years later, after the majestic building had fallen into disrepair, the Peiker family restored the mansion and opened it as Castle Marne, an inn that is now on the National Register of Historic Places.

By the front walk, an architecturally impressive Little Library, inspired by Castle Marne, welcomes guests. The look-alike Little Free Library features the same recognizable chimney, tower, and Peacock window, all on a small scale. It's lit at night, making the stained glass glow.

Three generations of Peikers steward the Little Free Library and run the bed and breakfast: Jim and Diane, daughter Missy and son-in-law Louie, and their three teenage grandchildren. The Little Library fits in with the sense of connection they want guests to experience. "We feel the Little Free Library itself engenders a sense and feeling of community," Jim says.

The doppelgänger Library gets regular visitors and donations, says Jim. "Located just a few blocks from downtown, we get a lot of foot traffic. Many folks stop and thank us for saving the old landmark mansion—as well as building a miniature reproduction," says Jim.

"Many folks stop and thank us for saving the old landmark mansion— as well as building a miniature reproduction."

—JIM PEIKER

MARGRET ALDRICH

ARTISTIC EXERCISES

Laura Damon-Moore—librarian, cofounder of the Library as Incubator Project, and coauthor of *The Artist's Library: A Field Guide* (Coffee House Press, 2014)—offers these three ideas for making art and stories based on Little Free Libraries. Some of the exercises are related to the stuff that's in the Little Libraries. Others are tied to the Libraries themselves. Grab a notebook, head to a nearby Little Free Library, and get inspired.

■ Have you found your nearest Little Free Library? Good. Examine it. Take note of what's inside the Little Library, and what's outside of it, too. Where is it located—in a yard, a park, by a path? Imagine this Library at night, at one or two in the morning. Who do you think would visit this particular Little Free Library at that time of night? Why? What are they looking for—if anything? Write down your ideas in your notebook. Draw a picture to accompany one of your ideas.

■ Close your eyes and pull out a book from the Little Free Library. Open your eyes. Remember, you can take this book with you if you would like. What is the title of this book? What is the cover like? Is it old or new? Read the first few pages. Smell the book. Does it have writing in it? Where do you think this book came from? Who was its most recent owner? What is this book's story? Write down your findings and ideas in your notebook. Draw a map of a possible route that the book took to get to this Little Library.

■ If the book you used for Exercise #2 is a chapter book, turn to one of the chapters in the middle of the book and search for a good "first sentence," a sentence that gets your brain thinking and compels you to continue the story, in your own words, from that point. If the book you picked is too short, or if there are no sentences in it that interest you, go back to the Little Library and find a new book to use. Write your story in your notebook for however long it interests you. And then write two more paragraphs.

Here are more ideas for creative exercises:

■ Host a Little Free Library design contest at your LFL. Ask patrons to draw the Little Free Library of their dreams—serious or fanciful—and submit their work to a designated folder in your Library. Kickstart their imaginations with starter questions like: What would your Little Free Library look like if it were made entirely of natural materials? Of pieces from an alien spacecraft? Of candy? What do you think the first Little Free Library in Antarctica should look like? What if an LFL were built at the bottom of the ocean or on the moon? Award prizes for first, second, and third places, and leave the drawings in a public folder in your Little Library for others to see.

■ Make small artworks and leave them in Little Free Libraries you encounter in your town or on your travels, along with a note that they should be taken. Whether the art piece is a sketch, a clay figure, or a stuffed nuigurumi, the finder will feel like he or she has uncovered a tiny treasure. Norbert Sarsfield and his thirteen-year-old daughter leave handmade bookmarks they call "Little Free Art" at the LFLs in their hometown of Iowa City, Iowa, and at other Little Libraries when on family trips. "We also like to leave bookmarks in public library books when we return them," Sarsfield says.

■ Draw a map of the Little Free Libraries in the area, highlighting landmarks, street signs, and businesses, as well as more creative details: Where is the prettiest spot to sit and read a book? What is the friendliest coffee shop? Where does the neighborhood stray cat like to hang out? Which Little Free Library is typically the fullest? Sketch out a suggested touring route, weaving a dotted line through the neighborhood map; if you'd like, use colored pencils to beautify your finished work. Make copies of your map and leave a small stack in each of the featured LFLs so patrons can easily find all the nearby Libraries.

CHAPTER 6

Make It Work

FINDING SOLUTIONS FOR CHALLENGING SITUATIONS

"*There's no use talking about the problem unless you talk about the solution.*"

—BETTY WILLIAMS

Little Free Libraries are typically problem free, with a steady influx of books and a loyal stream of patrons to help look after the neighborhood book exchanges. But every now and then, a steward faces a challenge that requires special attention. For some, that means attracting more visitors or drumming up more book donations; for others, it means getting a Little Free Library to a difficult location. For Hugh Kress, it meant replacing an entire Little Library after the structure was destroyed.

Kress had built a Little Free Library to stand in front of the tiny museum in the historical village of Rural, Wisconsin. Within a week, saboteurs had decimated the Library. "It was installed on a Friday, and the following Tuesday morning, I got a call from the neighbor next to the museum that the Library had been torched," Kress says. "Vandals firebombed and burned it and about thirty books to a pile of ashes." Not bowing to the sad event, Kress and other community members worked together to quickly rebuild the town's Little Library.

Although most predicaments aren't this extreme, bad things do happen to good Libraries. This chapter explores how stewards have overcome the challenges that sometimes arise with Little Free Libraries—or used the Libraries themselves to solve problems within their communities.

BRIAN, SARAH, AND SPENCER COLLINS

Leawood, Kansas, USA

Charter number: 11848

*D*angerous. *Threatening. Criminal.* These aren't words typically associated with a nine-year-old boy and his Little Free Library. That's why it caused such an uproar when the city of Leawood, Kansas, forced young Spencer Collins to take down the Little Free Library he had built with his dad and granddad as both a Mother's Day present for his mom, Sarah, and a way to engage with his neighborhood.

The cheery Little Library stood in Spencer's front yard, marked with the familiar cue to "Take a book." But because it was a freestanding structure, the Library violated a city code, and the Collins family received a notice telling them to remove it or be hit with a substantial fine.

Spencer was sad and confused when he heard the news. "I thought it was a good thing for the community, and I love reading," he says.

Almost immediately, Spencer's story went viral, causing public outcry. Everyone, it seemed, thought that Leawood had it wrong. "People from around the world reacted to the story," says Sarah. "We were overwhelmed by the support we received." The Collins family started a Facebook page for Spencer's Little Free Library, which quickly drew more than thirty thousand followers. The hashtag #FreeSpencersLibrary trended on social media. Hundreds of people contacted the Leawood City Council to request that the ordinance be amended to allow Little Free Libraries. And Spencer appeared on CNN, NPR, *The Today Show*, and more to talk about his outlawed Library.

In the midst of the kerfuffle, Spencer got a letter and book donation from children's author Daniel Handler—aka Lemony Snicket. It read:

Dear Mr. Collins,

It is my understanding that mysterious and sinister things have been occurring to your free library. Please consider these books a donation to your noble efforts and a warning to all mysterious and sinister people that fighting against librarians is immoral and useless in the face of brave and noble readers such as yourself.

With all due respect,
Lemony Snicket

He also received a touching note from Holocaust survivor and author Inge Auerbacher, who wrote, "Books are very important in life. I am a child survivor of the Holocaust, a time when the Nazis burned so many books. I would like to send you my first book, *I Am a Star,* because you are my little hero. You are my star. I was your age when I was in the concentration camp—without any books. God bless you."

As the next city council meeting approached, Spencer was determined to let his voice be heard and save his Little Free Library. The nine-year-old was full of common sense and brevity. "I want you to allow Little Free Libraries because I love to read," Spencer told the council. "Lots of people in the neighborhood used the Library, and the books were always changing. I think it's good for Leawood."

Kansas's poet laureate, Wyatt Townley, joined Spencer at the meeting and elegantly explained why she thinks Little Free Libraries are worth saving—not banning. "There's something about a Little Free Library, the intimacy of it . . . that as a small home for books, and as neighbor reaching out to neighbor, gives us something that a large library cannot," she said. "And so, I think we need more, not less, community in this day and age. I think we need more, not fewer, readers and thinkers in this day and age, and

I think that the Little Free Library addresses both these needs in a single, graceful gesture."

The decision was unanimous. The council ruled in favor of Spencer's Little Free Library (even though the person who made the initial complaint claimed that Little Libraries were eyesores that could house poisonous spiders or pornography). The council offered a temporary moratorium and pledged to find a permanent solution that would keep Little Free Libraries legal in Leawood, softening some of the national criticism they had received.

Spencer and his family were thrilled that they could reinstall their Library, and the town celebrated its return. "One of the best things after we put the Library back up was that people would drive down the street and honk or roll down the window and say how happy they were to see it," Sarah says.

Her advice to anyone else who runs into a problem with the law? "Begin the dialog with council people, explaining the benefit to the community," she says. "Show councils what other communities have done. Remember that it is a process and (I learned this from Spencer) don't be afraid to go to the council meeting to present your side."

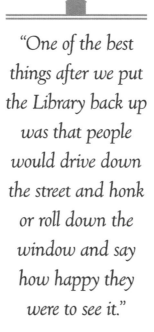

"One of the best things after we put the Library back up was that people would drive down the street and honk or roll down the window and say how happy they were to see it."

—SARAH COLLINS

JEANNE RATZLOFF

Kyangwali Refugee Settlement, Uganda, East Africa

Charter Number: 4996

The Kyangwali Refugee Settlement in western Uganda is home to twenty-five thousand displaced men, women, and children. Most are Congolese or Sudanese; others are refugees from Burundi, Ethiopia, Kenya, Rwanda, Somalia, and South Sudan. The site turns out to be a permanent home for many of the people who arrive here, though it's lacking in several basic necessities, like ample food, clean water, adequate medical care—and books.

A nonprofit group called PeopleWeaver is helping residents improve the social and economic conditions at the settlement by providing microcredit loans, school supplies, and more. When Jeanne Ratzloff, president of PeopleWeaver, realized the dearth of books, she also decided to bring a Little Free Library to the settlement's primary school—though establishing it would be a challenge.

"I have seen very few books in Kyangwali. I have never seen a child walking down one of the many dirt paths carrying a book. And I have never seen a book in one the many homes I've visited," Ratzloff says. "I have seen a few

adults with notebooks used for bookkeeping. I've seen a few children with school workbooks, although I haven't seen textbooks. Occasionally I've seen a homemade toy, but I've never seen a handmade book."

Since Kyangwali is isolated, and building materials would be difficult to get locally, Ratzloff and her colleagues made the Little Free Library stateside, then disassembled it, packed it in their baggage, and reassembled it when they reached Uganda. The shelving and wood were selected to be as lightweight as possible, but strong, and were packed alongside a shipment of reading glasses, provided through a partnership with EyeSee and ICU Eyewear.

"Our motto is 'one book at a time builds a library,'" Ratzloff says, and the Kyangwali Little Free Library now holds about two hundred books, mostly children's picture books. They hope to add more books for young adults in the future and build two more Little Libraries for the site.

"It is very, very hard for the parents in the camp to buy books for their children, because there is too much poverty. Almost every family lives on one dollar or less than one dollar a day," says Benson Wereje, the Ugandan project administrator. "This idea of the Little Free Library is great and important for these children, so they can learn and be exposed to ideas. A book is like gold; it is like lighting a fire."

DAVID CARR

Sandy Springs, Georgia, USA

Charter Number: 6357

When you open a Little Free Library door, it already feels like a treasure hunt, because there are always new books to discover inside. But the Lost Forest Little Free Library—which sits on a remote Georgia road—is so far off the beaten path, book seekers had trouble finding it. Now, patrons have an innovative map to follow: the Library is registered as an official geocaching site, bringing more visitors to its out-of-the way location.

Geocaching is an outdoor, recreational activity, where people program coordinates into a GPS device to search for little treasures hidden by other participants. There are more than two million active geocache sites and six million geocache hunters around the world. The prize at the terminus might be a note from the hider, a sticker, a small toy like an action figure, or, in this case, a Little Free Library.

The description for the Lost Forest Library on geocaching.com says: "The Lost Forest Little Free Library is a place for readers to find and take books, and return them when done. The library holds more than forty great books, all selected by a librarian and advocate for literacy. Messages may be left in a notebook attached to the library wall. The library is lighted, latched, and always open. Take a book, return a book."

Steward David Carr is happy to have geocachers visit his Library, a handsome, well-built structure finished in cedar stain. "There is not much pedestrian traffic where I live, so this added some lovely traffic and sweet comments."

Lucky geocachers find a carefully curated selection of books, already vetted by Carr, a former academic librarian and professor who says he sees libraries and museums as essential instruments of democracy.

"I rarely accept donations, because I want people to read things I know to be prizewinners, great reads, book club choices, or classics that maybe slipped past the reader," he says. "I have about a hundred books that I rotate in and out of the Library, usually eight or ten at a time, and I add more regularly." Each of those books has its own home-printed bookmark with an appropriate message like this one: "Reading is perhaps the greatest pleasure you will have in life; the one you will think of longest, and repent of least" (William Hazlitt).

The opening day booklist at the Lost Forest Little Free Library is impressive, making this a valuable cache for book lovers and one worth seeking out:

The Kitchen Boy	Robert Alexander
Possession	A. S. Byatt
One Shot	Lee Child
The Lincoln Lawyer	Michael Connelly
Homer and Langley	E. L. Doctorow
The Waterfall	Margaret Drabble
House of Sand and Fog	Andre Dubus III
Birdsong	Sebastian Faulks
A Passage to India	E. M. Forster
Second Wind	Dick Francis
In the Woods	Tana French
Complications	Atul Gawande
A Reliable Wife	Robert Goolrick
The Curious Incident of the Dog in the Night-Time	Mark Haddon
Jude the Obscure	Thomas Hardy
Plainsong	Kent Haruf
A Farewell to Arms	Ernest Hemingway
Finding Moon	Tony Hillerman
The Liar's Club	Mary Karr
Girl, Interrupted	Susanna Kaysen
A Question of Belief	Donna Leon
The Color of Water	James McBride
The Bluest Eye	Toni Morrison
Lost in America	Sherwin B. Nuland
The Things They Carried	Tim O'Brien
Bel Canto	Ann Patchett
The Greatest Thing Since Sliced Bread	Don Robertson
Chosen Prey	John Sandford
Murder Must Advertise	Dorothy L. Sayers
The Killer Angels	Michael Shaara
Shane	Jack Shaefer
The Pianist	Wladyslaw Szpilman
The Good War	Studs Terkel
The Daughter of Time	Josephine Tey
A Test of Wills	Charles Todd
This Boy's Life	Tobias Wolff

SCOTT, STACEY, NAOMI, AND SARAH PORTER

Rancho Palos Verdes, California, USA

Charter Number: 6767

When a Little Free Library was stolen from its perch in the Porter family's front yard, their small town rallied to show support and help rebuild. Here, Stacey explains how—through the misfortune of a missing Library—she was heartened by the generosity of her community.

"The story of our Library must begin with the story of how it was inspired.

In March of 2012, my mother passed away after a very short battle with pancreatic cancer. She was young and it was surprise to all of us, as she died only twenty-nine days after her diagnosis.

My mother was a hoarder of high-end sewing and quilting notions. Upon her death, she left all of her collection to me. Unfortunately, I am not a seamstress, quilter, or crafter. For a year, I just closed the doors to her sewing rooms—it was too painful to look at her dreams.

In February of 2013, though, my daughters and I decided to start selling my mother's collection. We opened an eBay business and sold software, notions,

thread, and fabric to customers all over the world. Our eBay store is called "My Mother's Dreams," and it felt good to get her dreams into the hands of people who could use them.

As we watched our profit grow, I told my daughters that we must do something really good with the proceeds of our sales *before* we started to do something indulgent. Thus, the Little Free Library became the good that we would use the money for. We splurged on a four-hundred-dollar Library, and felt happy to use the money from selling my mother's dreams to fund our little dream of having a Little Library in front of our home.

For six weeks my family enjoyed being stewards of the Library. We have frequent Girl Scout and church meetings at our home, so our Library saw lots of use. We also have international exchange students who live with us, so we stocked books in many languages for them to use. My daughters wrote personal notes in each book, telling readers why they liked particular books.

Then, one evening in late October, our neighbor knocked on our door with an armful of books. I opened the door with a huge smile, thinking that our neighbor was making a donation of books. Our smiles turned quickly to tears as the neighbor told us that someone had stolen our Library and thrown the books on the lawn.

I wanted to teach my children that it is important to take action when something bad happens to you. We immediately contacted the police, who arrived at our home within fifteen minutes. They recorded the details of the story, but we knew there was little hope of recovering the Library.

I encouraged my children to write a letter to the editor of the Palos Verdes newspaper to alert neighbors and community residents of our loss. Perhaps someone may have seen something? Perhaps this was a teenage prank, and maybe the teenager would toss it into a canyon and it would be found? The editor contacted me immediately and wanted to interview us for a front-page story.

Over the course of the weeks following the theft, many neighbors stopped by to tell us how sad they were that our Library was stolen. They offered condolences and encouraged us to rebuild it and not let a thief steal something that was so good for our community.

After the story was published, we had an overwhelming response. The Friends of the Palos Verdes Library offered to restock our Library if it was found or rebuilt. The Book Frog, a local bookstore, offered discounts to anyone who wanted to purchase books for our Library. Private citizens offered to help finance the rebuilding of our Library. And William Weisinger, a retired engineer from St. Peter's by the Sea Presbyterian Church, offered to rebuild the Library for us!

The Porter family is full of gratitude for the support of our Palos Verdes community. Mr. Weisinger rebuilt our Library structure using materials that were being discarded from the homes he builds for low-income residents of Los Angeles. As we worked with Mr. Weisinger to dig the post hole and pour concrete to secure the Library, we had several drivers stop and praise our efforts. When you live in a small town, people rally behind you to turn something bad into something good. We are honored to have our roles as community librarians restored, and we will do our best to stock the Library's shelves with meaningful books. "

VANDALISM AND OTHER CONCERNS

If you ask the Little Free Library team, "Won't someone vandalize our Library?" their answer is, "Maybe . . . but probably not." Reports of vandalism are few and far between. However, rushes of youthful energy—or alcohol—can make a Little Free Library a tempting target. To keep yours safe, follow these tips.

■ Install your Little Free Library in a well-lit area. The more a vandal thinks he'll get caught, the less likely he is to cause mischief.

■ Make it beautiful. A well-designed, well-kept Library that is clearly looked after and valued is less likely to be tagged or otherwise vandalized. Keep the paint fresh and the surrounding landscaping free of weeds and trash.

■ If you'll be out of town for an extended period, ask a neighbor to look after your Little Free Library. In addition to keeping it tidy, they can alert you if any problems arise.

■ Make it clear that your Little Free Library belongs to the neighborhood. Post a sign that says, "Thank you for protecting and loving our Library!" A message like this, showing that people care about the Library, can deter troublemakers.

■ Believe in the goodness of strangers. "For just about every story of damage to Little Free Libraries, we've heard others that inspire us," the Little Free Library team says. "The wounded Libraries were mysteriously repaired or replaced, or we've found donors to rebuild them. And in one case, the perpetrator wasn't kids or gangs. It was mother nature herself!" A Little Free Library that was covered with metal keys for decoration was struck by lightning—not vandals.

Other concerns from Little Free Library stewards:

What if my city won't let me install a Little Free Library?

While it's rare for a municipality to prohibit Little Free Libraries based on zoning laws, it's not unheard of. In 2012, the village board in Whitefish Bay, Wisconsin, deemed Little Free Libraries unfit for front yards. (Backyards, fine—but isn't that missing the point?) And in 2014, Spencer Collins made national news when he was forced to take down his Little Library in Leawood, Kansas (read the whole story on page 156). In both cases, the rulings were reversed after the decision makers got to know more about Little Free Libraries.

Make your Library welcome in any neighborhood by following a few simple guidelines: For the easiest route, choose a spot on your personal property rather than on public property. If you want to locate your Little Free Library on public ground—such as a park, schoolyard, or other shared area—you'll need to clear it with the appropriate officials first. In either case, be sure the Little Library doesn't interfere with other people's activities, such as walking, biking, or shoveling snow; give it an attractive design; keep it well maintained; and make sure that the construction is solid and the Library is safely anchored.

If your town does have rules against freestanding structures, follow Spencer's advice: Don't be afraid to talk with your local government. Once they know the benefits of Little Free Libraries, they are likely to welcome them to the community.

What if someone steals all my books?

The books in Little Free Libraries are meant to be taken, but if your Library is cleaned out in one fell swoop, it feels like a violation. If you suspect someone

is pilfering your Library and reselling the books, remind them that the inventory is meant to be shared freely among the community: Buy a stamp from Little Free Library that reads "Always a Gift, Never for Sale," or print a label that says, "Not for resale. This is a free book," and mark each book to dissuade used bookstores from buying them. Post a notice in your Library that reads, "Taking all the books ruins this Library for everyone. Please leave books for others." Ask neighbors to help watch over the Library. Or register your books on bookcrossing.com, a website that lets bibliophiles track their books to see where they end up. (This can be a fun thing to do anyway.)

Will some neighbors have a problem with my Little Free Library?

Most people seem to love Little Free Libraries, especially if you make it clear that the Library is for everyone. Invite the entire neighborhood to enjoy your Little Library (see ideas in "Launching Your Library" on page 54). Note that your neighbors shouldn't be worried by the extra foot traffic on your street—more pedestrians on the sidewalk can mean less crime.

Don't Little Free Libraries devalue books, shut down bookstores, and take jobs from public librarians?

The short answer? No. Little Free Libraries contribute to a thriving culture of literacy. Chances are, devotees of your Little Library are also regulars at the bookstore and enthusiastic public library-goers. (Most bibliophiles say you can't have too many books.) In addition, Little Free Libraries can encourage nonreaders to pick up a book—or two, or three—and introduce kids to a love of reading.

What if inappropriate materials show up in my Little Free Library?

While banning books isn't in the spirit of Little Free Libraries, you should curate your Library in a way that makes you comfortable. Books that are beat up and falling apart should certainly be culled. Most stewards choose to pull out the religious pamphlets that sometimes show up. And if you don't want hot-blooded romance novels—where all the men have hairless chests and all the plots are poorly written—by all means, yank them.

To find answers to other frequently asked questions, visit littlefreelibrary.org/faqs.

LOS ANGELES POLICE DEPARTMENT

Los Angeles, California, USA

Charter Number: 10271 and others

Heading down to the police station doesn't have to be a bad thing, especially if you live in the city of Los Angeles. The LAPD is installing Little Free Libraries in their stations to soften the precincts' hard, gritty reputations; promote youth literacy; and develop better relationships with the public.

Building trust between residents and local police departments is key to a healthy community, says Captain Robert Arcos, Seventy-Seventh Street Area Commanding Officer. "A police station is often viewed as a very sterile environment. A place to report crimes, visit loved ones in jail, seek assistance for troubled teens or other family members—all in all not a positive experience," he says. "Therefore the more opportunities we create to have a positive experience, the better we connect to our communities."

The first LAPD-sponsored Little Free Library opened in South L.A. at the Seventy-Seventh Area Station in 2013. Officers host readings for kids, tours, book drives, and other events to invite the public to the station to get to know the

officers. In addition, the Libraries help introduce kids to LAPD's free youth activities, such as the Cadet and Jr. Cadet programs, which teach life skills, leadership, and civic responsibility.

"The community response has been overwhelming," says Captain Robert Arcos. "The Little Free Library in the Seventy-Seventh Street Division is constantly in use. We have book readings by police officers every other week highlighting the LFL experience. Elementary school tours are conducted twice a month, and each tour includes a book reading by officers from a Little Free Library book."

Since the original LAPD Little Free Library was installed, several additional Libraries have opened in sites including the LAPD Pacific Area Community Police Station, which serves the Venice Beach community; the LAPD Olympic Area Community Station, which serves the Pico Union and Koreatown area; the LAPD Foothill Area Community Police Station; the Hollenbeck Area Station,

and the LAPD Topanga Area Community Police Station in the Valley. The force plans to install twenty-one Little Free Libraries in all, one for each of LAPD's geographic areas.

Senior Lead Officer Heidi Stoecklein says, "Our goals are simple. The LAPD wants to help to promote literacy and the love of reading by building a safe place for young people in the neighborhood to have free book exchanges. We are also building a sense of community and allowing young people to see LAPD officers as real people."

MARGRET ALDRICH

JIM BOSWELL

Carrizozo, New Mexico, USA

Charter Number: 2428 and others

The dusty, desert town of Carrizozo, New Mexico—population 1,100—doesn't have a hospital, movie theater, or mall. It's the neighbor to a handful of abandoned ghost towns. And it has never had a public library. But the hamlet's small stature won't keep its citizens from reading books: Carrizozo is the proud home to thirteen Libraries . . . the little, free kind.

Five Little Free Libraries are already part of the town's cactus-studded landscape, and eight more are in the works, says steward Jim Boswell. "I'm a heavy reader, and after moving here in 2010, I became frustrated with library access," he says. (With good reason: Billy the Kid's old stomping grounds are a stone's throw from Carrizozo, but the closest public library is thirty miles away.)

"A longtime friend turned me on to Little Free Libraries, and in August 2012 I launched the first one in town." Soon after, Carrizozo Works, a local community-development group, agreed to fund and promote more Libraries through its Adopt-a-Block program, helping raise $5,800 in grants.

When all thirteen installations are done, Carrizozo "might just be the smallest town with the most Little Free Libraries per capita," Boswell says.

What Carrizozo lacks in size, though, it makes up for in community involvement—hosting rodeos, art shows, street fairs, motorcycle rallies, and more—and the townspeople have embraced the Little Free Library movement with the same enthusiasm and camaraderie. To help them carry books between the well-used Libraries, Boswell has ambitious plans to make and give away a thousand tote bags: one for each resident.

The small, book-loving town is also in the process of establishing a traditional public library—one with reading chairs, late fees, and bookshelves to the ceiling—which will bring Carrizozo's total to fourteen. Pretty soon, libraries will outnumber the tumbleweeds.

The Little Free Library organization supports efforts like Carrizozo's through its Little Free Libraries for Small Towns initiative, which funds Little Libraries in towns that don't have brick-and-mortar public libraries of their own. Supporters can contact the organization to sponsor Little Libraries, and small towns can apply to receive one. "There are eleven thousand U.S. towns with no library," says Little Free Library cofounder Todd Bol. "We think that's kind of a crime."

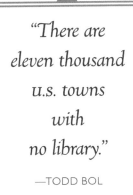

"There are eleven thousand U.S. towns with no library."

—TODD BOL

WHEN BOOKS GET STALE

You know the type. They overstay their welcome, sitting in the corner and taking up space. Whether it's an Italian travel guide from 1982 or a Spam cookbook, sometimes you have to ask a book to leave. By clearing out books that have lingered on your Little Free Library shelf for too long, you can make room for titles that visitors will be excited to take home. But don't fret: there are creative ways to use those misfit books and give them new life.

Pass it on
Is it a good book in good condition that just hasn't found the right reader? Donate it to another Little Free Library, secondhand store, or school library, where an appreciative reader might find it.

Make book art
Book pages can be cut and transformed into paper flowers, wreaths, and picture frames; book covers can become storage boxes and handbags. Look at *The Repurposed Library* by Lisa Occhipinti, *Playing with Books* by Jason Thompson, *Book Art* by Clare Youngs, or Pinterest for book-craft inspiration.

Create a book safe
Carve out the inside of an unwanted hardcover book, leave a note or object inside, and place it in your Little Free Library for the next visitor to discover. Ask them to take the book home and put another note or object inside, then return the book to the Little Library for someone else to find.

Reuse the pages
Tear out book pages and use them to decoupage the inside of your Little Free Library, as wrapping paper for small gifts, or as origami paper. Leave origami creations in your Library for patrons to find and take home.

CHRISTINE MIHOCK AND TARA RYAN, HOPE FOR HIGHLANDS

Highlands, New Jersey, USA

Charter Number: 4764

In October 2012, Hurricane Sandy devastated the East Coast. It was the largest storm the Atlantic seaboard had ever seen, spanning 1,100 miles and causing $68 billion in damage. The small waterfront fishing village of Highlands, on New Jersey's northeastern coast, was hit especially hard, says resident Christine Mihok: "Twelve hundred of 1,500 homes were destroyed and had to be demolished or rebuilt, and raised to avoid future flood waters. The Highlands Boro Library, located in the community center, was also destroyed, along with every other boro[ugh] building."

The volunteer-run library had been open three days a week and was the blue-collar community's only local spot for reading, doing research, and borrowing books. But reopening the Boro Library wasn't the priority in a village that had to rebuild so many homes and roads. Mihok's solution? Bring a Little Free Library to Highlands to both share books and serve as a small harbor from the town's hardships.

With no resources to start the Library, Mihok—through the nonprofit group Hope for Highlands—applied for support through Little Free Library's GIFT Fund. Soon the Highlands Little Free Library was established across from a quiet park, near four of the first local shops to reopen after Superstorm Sandy. "It looks like a little house growing out of a planter," says Mihok. "People sitting at tables outside a nearby coffee shop, or those stopping to rent a bicycle to tour the town, may not notice the Little Free Library right away, but when they do, they are delighted. It gives a much-needed smile to many, especially families with children."

Although the public library has yet to reopen after the havoc of Hurricane Sandy, the town's Little Free Library fills the gap in a small but significant way. "We were fortunate to be recipients of the GIFT program," Mihok says. "The residents of Highlands love the LFL. It has fostered conversation and discussion and is a very bright note in a tough little town that is fighting to come back from a natural disaster."

"The Little Free Library has given Highlands a sense of hope," she continues. "Perhaps seeing this bright little house rising up from the devastation has encouraged our citizens, showing that they too can rise up."

"Perhaps seeing this bright little house rising up from the devastation has encouraged our citizens, showing that they too can rise up."

—CHRISTINE MIHOCK

JOHN KIELTYKA AND MONIKA LIDMAN

Seattle, Washington, USA

Charter Number: 12012

KAREN AND BOB WHITE

Seattle, Washington, USA

Charter Number: 11331

Same city. Same block. Same day.

John Kieltyka and Monika Lidman of Seattle, Washington, had been hard at work building their Little Free Library and were excited to share it. What they didn't know was that neighbors Karen and Bob White were building one, too. When the two couples carried their Libraries to their front yards for installation, they witnessed what Lidman calls "a lovely bit of synchronicity."

"Monika and I had no idea at all that Karen and Bob were planning the same thing," says Kieltyka. "I had been quietly toiling away on our Library through the rainy Seattle winter, and once done, I waited for a clear day to bring out the Library. So did Karen and Bob!"

Within an hour of each other, both Little Free Libraries on the 4800 block of Rutan Place SW—now called the best-read street in Seattle—were open for business. But don't expect a turf war between the Libraries. "We definitely don't think there can be too many Little Free Libraries in one neighborhood," says Kieltyka. "In fact, a big topic of conversation the day we installed our simultaneous boxes was about what it would take to get every house on our little dead-end street to put one up. It was generally agreed to be a great idea."

Having more than one Library on the block has provided some real advantages, Kieltyka says, including more visitors: "We love interacting with our neighborhood and always enjoy meeting new neighbors. This has increased as more people have learned about the 'dueling' Libraries on our street."

"I think people enjoy 'shopping' at both. We can offer more books than a single Little Free Library can," says Karen White, who also enjoys visiting her neighbors' Library. "I've taken several books out of John and Monika's, as have family members. (And I've told them that if I find a book in my Library that I don't like, I'll put it in theirs!)"

THE NOT-SO-NEW LIBRARY

Don't let your Little Free Library disappear into the background after its novelty wears off. Small details can infuse it with energy, keep it humming with visitors, and ensure that it stays packed with books. Try one or more of these ideas to reinvigorate your Little Library after the honeymoon period and keep readers coming back.

Take a seat
Many stewards say that installing a bench next to your Little Free Library will double the number of people that stop and linger. Sturdy lawn chairs or even well-placed logs will also encourage people to sit a moment as they thumb through a book or start a conversation.

Book bonuses
Include surprise materials inside the books in your Library, like a recipe, personal note, poem (written by you or someone else), bookmark, review of the book, or a hand-drawn map of other Little Free Libraries in the area. Or make library cards to give out in your Library for patrons to keep in their wallets as a reminder that their friendly neighborhood Little Free Library is always open.

Keep it fresh
If visitors see the same old books every time they stop by your Little Free Library, they're bound to get bored—and stop coming back. Refresh your books often. By pulling out the books that languish and replacing them with something new, you'll add a sense of discovery back to your Library. (Feel free to gradually return the old books to the Library. After a few weeks on hiatus, they'll seem new again.)

Open call
Find creative ways to let neighbors know that book donations are needed. For example, try adding a mailbox flag to the side of your Library. To announce that you're running low on books, put the flag in the "up" position.

MARGRET ALDRICH

Add audio

For an instant soundtrack, set up a music box in your Little Free Library that is tripped whenever someone opens the door. Or find a motion-activated toy that lets you record a message for visitors, like "Welcome to our Little Free Library" or "Steal this book."

Keep track

Do you wonder how many people are using your Little Free Library? Install a counter in your Library, so you'll know how many times its door is opened each day. (See page 244 of the appendix for detailed instructions.) Keep track of ebbs and flows in Little Library traffic. What patterns do you see?

Grand (re)opening

Remember that you can introduce your Library to the neighborhood more than once. Get people excited about it again by revisiting the activities mentioned in "Launching Your Library" on page 54. Instead of a ribbon-cutting celebration, host a block party at your Little Library; or think of new stories to share with your local newspaper.

Do Good

USING LITTLE FREE LIBRARIES TO PAY IT FORWARD

"We all do better
when we all
read better."

—LITERACY FRIENDLY

NEIGHBORHOOD PROJECT

CHAPTER 7
DO GOOD

How can you use a Little Free Library as a force for good in the world? In essence, any Little Free Library is doing something positive, just by being: they naturally foster closer community ties, promote literacy and a love of reading, and inspire creativity and a sharing culture. But some Little Free Libraries take special care to pay it forward.

Hundreds of Little Free Libraries have been erected as "legacy Libraries," for example—built in remembrance of loved ones who have died, as a way for their memories to live on. Many have been built to bring books to people and places in need, whether in our backyard or overseas. And others have been built to encourage communities going through hard times, standing as small beacons of renewal, progress, and hope.

The Little Free Library stewards featured in this chapter are often surprised at the powerful effect their Little Libraries can have on others. Read their accounts and discover how you can help your neighborhood—and the Little Free Library movement—thrive.

INMATES OF THE PRAIRIE DU CHIEN CORRECTIONAL INSTITUTE

Prairie du Chien, Wisconsin, USA

Charter Number: Multiple

"It's a very positive place for gathering."

—SHARON ADAMS

Little Free Libraries are forged in a variety of places: They're pieced together in well-stocked workshops, jerry-rigged in sunny backyards, or lovingly made at Little Free Library headquarters itself. Others are hammered and sanded in a more secure spot—behind the bars of the Prairie du Chien Correctional Institute.

Through a partnership between the Wisconsin Department of Corrections and Little Free Library, prisoners in the Goodmates program build Little Libraries in their building-maintenance and construction class. Using donated or recycled materials—scrap wood from pallets, plexiglass, handles, and hinges—inmates have free reign to design and build the Little Free Library they envision, from brightly painted boxes to miniature log cabins. When the Libraries are done, they're given to communities in need across the United States.

Beyond gaining the satisfaction of giving back, inmates learn valuable design, carpentry, and construction skills (if on a small scale) that can help them secure jobs after they're released. They also pick up an appreciation for books, perhaps for the first time. According to the state of Wisconsin's "Read to Lead" program, 40 percent of their inmates enter prison without a high school diploma, and 7 percent read below a fourth-grade level.

The program has been hugely successful, and more than a hundred Little Libraries have been constructed at Prairie du Chien. In large part, the prison has correctional officer Patricia Bailey to thank. After Patti and her husband erected their own Little Free Library in 2011, she immediately thought LFLs would be a great project for the inmates, and she drew up a proposal for the prison's warden and legal counsel. Lightning quick, the project got the green light. "The warden made a comment he has never seen anything get approved as fast as this," Bailey says.

When a Goodmates Library is finished, it is gifted to a place where it can be of service. Several have made their way to the Lindsay Heights neighborhood of Milwaukee—an area that currently encompasses the two poorest zip codes in the city but is on its way to revitalization. One stands in the garden of the Walnut Way Conservation Corp., a nonprofit devoted to spurring civic engagement in the Lindsay Heights community.

The inmate-built Libraries are already making a difference. "Yesterday, I visited our Little Free Library, and a young neighbor helped me refresh it and add more books. We read together," says Walnut Way cofounder Sharon Adams. "It's a very positive place for gathering."

HOW YOU CAN HELP

It takes a lot of extra support to keep the Little Free Library organization going. The tiny staff manages hundreds of new Little Free Libraries, two hundred thousand website visitors, and four hundred thousand Facebook views every month. The nonprofit runs on a shoestring budget. And there are many places around the world that still need Little Libraries.

Become an advocate for the Little Free Library movement—and spread the word—by following one or more of the prompts below. And thank you for the kind support you've already shared.

- You can't beat the basics: Build a Little Free Library for your front yard. Contribute a book to someone else's Little Free Library. And try out some of the exercises in this book to help build literacy, community, and creativity in your neighborhood.

- Donations are crucial to the survival and continued success of Little Free Library. Give what you can online, and your money will help keep the organization running, build Libraries, and fund programs like Books around the Block, Friends through the Years, and Good Global Neighbors.

- Money isn't the only thing you can donate to the cause. Other helpful items include vehicles for hauling books and Little Free Libraries; frequent flyer miles, to help fund the travel required for building the network of Little Free Libraries; gas station gift cards; printing services, for mailings and instructional materials; and computer equipment for the Little Free Library offices.

- Tell someone about Little Free Libraries and the mission of the project. Better yet, take them to a Little Library and show them how they work. Even better, offer to teach them how to build a Little Free Library, or help them install one in their front yard.

- Gather colleagues, friends, or family members and build one or more Little Free Libraries. Donate them to an area book desert, where public libraries and bookstores are out of reach. To orchestrate a larger-scale endeavor, see "Organizing a Community Build Day" on page 206.

- Bring a Little Free Library to your local school, using funding provided by the PTA or Little Free Library–sponsored programs like Books around the Block. Alternatively, build a Library to auction at a school function, and use the funds to buy new books for the school's library.

- If your town has a farmer's market, summer carnival, or annual community showcase, set up a Little Free Library information booth. Display a Little Library, if possible, so people can see one up close, and hand out basic brochures. Ask community members where they would like to see a Little Free Library located, and offer a sign-up sheet for those who want to help make it happen.

- Organize an event to raise money for local nonprofits concerned with literacy. Participants could include publishers, public libraries, writing centers, independent bookstores, tutoring groups, and Little Free Library supporters. Host author readings, a silent auction, and a book exchange at the event; ask neighborhood caterers and brewers to donate food and drink; and screen the documentary *Because It's Small: The Story of the Little Free Library Movement.*

- If you'll be traveling to a remote part of the world, explore whether you can install a Little Free Library while you're there. LFL supporter David Laufer, for example, packed materials for a Little Free Library as part of his baggage when he flew to Jakarta, Indonesia, where it was enthusiastically embraced. College students from the University of Madison–Wisconsin have ushered them into Nepal and Kenya.

    "The model works well," says cofounder Rick Brooks. "Take one. Show people how easy they are to build. Encourage them to build them in their local style and with cultural relevance. If possible, find a partner school or community group here in the U.S., so both sides of the partnership can share what they value with their new friends halfway around the world."

LISA HEYDLAUFF

Patna, Bihar, India

Charter Number: Multiple

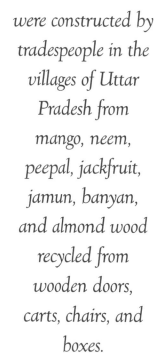

The Little Libraries were constructed by tradespeople in the villages of Uttar Pradesh from mango, neem, peepal, jackfruit, jamun, banyan, and almond wood recycled from wooden doors, carts, chairs, and boxes.

How do you teach young people to become entrepreneurs when they live in low-income areas with few role models to follow? Tell them a story. Going to School, a nonprofit education trust in India, uses the power of storytelling to inspire underprivileged students to grow into successful businesspeople and problem solvers.

Going to School creates "Be! Books"—story-driven graphic novels that teach key entrepreneurial skills, such as leadership, identifying a problem, making a plan, budgeting, and negotiating, as well as the importance of being on time, building relationships, and communicating effectively. In addition, the stories teach the importance of staying in school.

Statistics show that 50 percent of children in India do not finish school, 300 million citizens are illiterate, and 250 million live in dire poverty. Going to School hopes to change those numbers, student by student. "We're currently working in 871 secondary schools teaching more than eighty-seven thousand children in Grade 9 imperative skills at school," says Lisa Heydlauff, chief executive officer of Going to School. "Girls ages twelve to fourteen are over 50 percent of our audience. They love the stories and excel in the weekend skills challenges and projects they have to complete."

Now Little Free Libraries are going to school, too. As part of the program, Heydlauff is working to bring one thousand Little Free Libraries to India's schools and fill them with Be! Books. The first twelve of these Libraries were installed in the twelve highest-performing classrooms, and now the skill stories are available to students anytime. "We deliver over two hundred books of all sizes to schools each year, and we know that there is no place to keep them, so they are often kept in the headmistress's office," says Heydlauff. "We wanted to make sure the books were accessible to children in the program, whenever they needed them—that's why we built the Little Free Libraries. The students love them."

The Little Libraries were constructed by tradespeople in the villages of Uttar Pradesh from mango, neem, peepal, jackfruit, jamun, banyan, and almond wood recycled from wooden doors, carts, chairs, and boxes. It took three days for them to travel to Bihar, where they were tied with red bows before they were presented to the classrooms.

Teachers and Going to School administrators hope the Little Free Libraries and the inspirational stories inside of them will help students reach their fullest potential. "Every child has talent," says Prerna Kumari, a teacher at Sarvodaya High School in the Nalanda District of Bihar. "Through Be! Stories, I've found a way to help children discover the skills hidden inside of them."

LINDA PROUT

New Orleans, Louisiana, USA

Charter Number: 194

Hurricane Katrina was one of the most devastating natural disasters in U.S. history, flooding 80 percent of the city of New Orleans and obliterating many of its beloved neighborhoods. In its humble way, Linda Prout's Little Free Library—the first one in Louisiana—played a small but mighty part in bringing a sense of community back to the city, as it inspired a domino effect of good works.

Tell us about your Little Free Library and how it inspired more Little Free Libraries in New Orleans.

Our family's love affair with Little Free Libraries started with an e-mail. In October of 2011, a friend sent our daughter Jennifer a link to a Minnesota *Star Tribune* newspaper article about Little Free Libraries, and Jennifer forwarded it to me. Totally smitten, I immediately ordered one to give to my husband Lee for Christmas. We invited neighbors to come to our Library's grand opening on the first Saturday in December 2011. They introduced themselves, ate king cake and drank lemonade, and went home with new books to read. The Tall Timbers Little Free Library has been a well-used and greatly appreciated part of the neighborhood ever since. But I had no idea what a huge impact it would have on my life.

The Little Free Library organization saw pictures of our grand opening on Facebook and offered to build a very special Little Library for New Orleans, to support the city's recovery from the devastation of Hurricane Katrina and the flooding that followed. Its theme would be "Coming Together in New Orleans," to celebrate that the city had not just survived Katrina, but was thriving because of the way people were working together to rebuild. The theme was explained through the artwork of a local artist and text by a local writer, both of which were engraved on granite panels on the Library. People from all over town wrote letters telling why they wanted the donated Library and what it would do for their neighborhood. Amazingly, the judges (First Lady Cheryl Landrieu, civil rights activist Ruby Bridges, and City Librarian Charles Brown) all chose the same letter, and the Little Library was installed at a home in Faubourg St. John.

Then the mayor's office offered "Love Your Block" grants for projects to improve your neighborhood. Our church applied for a grant to build and install ten Little Free Libraries in neighborhoods throughout New Orleans, picking ten more new stewards from the letters that had already been written for the project

described above. We received the grant, but the catch was that we had to build and install the Libraries, and submit the final report with "before and after" pictures, in thirty days! A lot of people did not think it was possible, but we did it. Over fifty volunteers, including preschoolers, Boy Scouts, youth group members, and adults worked together to build the plywood inner boxes and then cover them with Katrina debris from the Green Project (a nonprofit organization that recycles building supplies from demolished houses). Boy Scouts dug the postholes and did the installation, and we finished with time to spare.

And then, during the 2012–13 school year, artist Stephan Wanger painted four Little Free Libraries with pictures of Louisiana flowers (hibiscus, bird-of-paradise, magnolia, and camellia). I served as the Glue Gun Chick while the students at Audubon Charter School cut apart strings of Mardi Gras beads and then glued the beads on one at a time until the Libraries were completely covered. Each Library took us two months to complete and toured Louisiana as part of a Bead Town art exhibit. We are planning to work on Louisiana iris and pitcher plant Libraries next.

How have the Libraries had an impact on your community?
Ripples from Little Free Libraries continue to spread throughout New Orleans.

- Friends of the New Orleans Public Library (FNOPL) donated over one hundred boxes of children's books to Library stewards.
- Freshmen at Xavier University built two Little Free Libraries for their Gert Town neighborhood.
- Nikki, a seven-year-old steward, received a Disney grant to fund a book-donating and -swapping party, and then to buy books at the FNOPL book sale for the next eighteen months.
- A Girl Scout troop in Metairie built and installed two Libraries to earn the Silver Award.
- A civic association hosted a "Bring a Book, a Buck, or Both" event to purchase and supply a neighborhood Library.
- A Little Free Library filled with gardening books was installed in the camellia garden at Latter Library in memory of civic activist Diana Pinckley.
- A steward in the Irish Channel neighborhood holds monthly storytelling events for children at her Library.
- Two community gardens have installed Little Free Libraries.
- Barnes and Noble in Gretna, Louisiana, chose Little Free Library as their holiday book-drive recipient, and customers bought and donated two thousand new children's books that were given to Little Libraries in New Orleans.

As you can see, the possibilities are endless.

What books are in your Tall Timbers–neighborhood Little Free Library right now?

Our motto is "Something for Everyone." So we always try to have books on cooking, gardening, dogs, home repair, and New Orleans, some best sellers for adults, popular series for older children, lots of picture books, and a few board books for the babies. Titles currently available include *Zeitoun*, *The Immortal Life of Henrietta Lacks*, *Mockingjay*, *Cooking Chinese*, *Wild Flowers*, *Marley & Me*, *Captain Underpants*, *Corduroy*, *The Cat in the Hat*, and the *Goodnight Moon* board book.

What is the weirdest book (or other item) that has shown up in your Little Free Library?

Our weirdest books came when Tracy Mumford, the steward of the Headless Little Free Library in Minneapolis (page 144), suggested an interlibrary exchange: five New Orleans books for five Minnesota books. We sent *Gumbo Tales: Finding My Place at the New Orleans Table*, *Hurricane Song*, *Heavenly Delight* by the Kitchen Krewe of Gretna United Methodist Church, *Go Out and Play: Favorite Outdoor Games from KaBOOM!*, and *1 Dead in Attic: After Katrina*. In return, we received *Boundary Waters*, *Lake Wobegon Summer 1956*, *Blue Ribbon Winners: America's Best State Fair Recipes*, *Roofwalker*, and *Spam: A Biography*.

Is there anything else you want to share about your experience with Little Free Libraries?

Here are the top three reasons why I love the Little Free Library organization:

1. Each Little Library is a blank slate and allows people to share their passions with others—gardening, health and fitness, cooking, construction, mysteries, literacy for young children . . .

2. In New Orleans, 80 percent of the people lost everything after Katrina and had to rebuild homes, schools, churches, libraries, playgrounds, and businesses. They have a strong attachment to their neighborhoods and use Little Free Libraries as community centers where they can talk to their neighbors and continue to find ways to work together to make improvements.

3. The New Orleans Public Library Foundation states that 44 percent of the people in New Orleans are functionally illiterate. Their current goal is to work to make New Orleans the most literate city in the country, and having books available in Little Free Libraries in every neighborhood will certainly help to achieve that goal.

"Students at Audubon Charter School cut apart strings of Mardi Gras beads and then glued the beads on one at a time until the Libraries were completely covered."

MARGRET ALDRICH

TINA SIPULA

Bloomington, Illinois, USA

Charter Number: 2056

The Clare House is a food pantry that gives out more than groceries. It provides books, too. "Nearly eighty people gather in front of our house twice a week for food, and many use our Little Free Library," says Tina Sipula, who runs the food pantry, as well as a soup kitchen at a nearby church.

"The homeless do not have an address, so they cannot get a library card at our public library," Sipula says. "I wanted a Little Free Library in front of our food pantry so the many who come to us in need of food could have the opportunity to have free books for themselves and for their children. It's very active, with people coming to pick up books and people dropping them off. It changes daily."

One volunteer named Bill Tolone collects 150 children's books a week for Clare House and distributes them in the food line. Books in the Little Library have included *The Golden Compass* by Philip Pullman, *The Karate Kid* by B. B. Hiller, and *Harry Potter and the Chamber of Secrets* by J. K. Rowling, as well as titles for adult readers, like *She's Come Undone* by Wally Lamb, *Nights in Rodanthe* by

MARGRET ALDRICH

Nicholas Sparks, *A Tree Grows in Brooklyn* by Betty Smith, and *Working Words*, an anthology edited by M. L. Liebler.

Sipula is happy to provide Clare House visitors with books—no library card required. "I come from a family of eight children and grew up in Ottawa, Illinois, where my father was a factory worker. My whole life I loved to read, and we could not afford many books, so I went to the library a lot," she says.

HELEN CRARY STASSEN AND JAY STASSEN

Prescott, Wisconsin, USA

Charter Number: 260

In the best cases, our heartbreaks can be transformed into something meaningful. After parents Helen and Jay Stassen lost their son Benjamin, a Little Free Library overlooking the peaceful St. Croix and Mississippi Rivers became a healing memorial.

What is your Little Free Library's story? Why did you decide to build it, and what makes it special?

Our youngest son Benjamin died tragically in October of 2010. Benjamin was a twenty-one-year-old college student, and he died by suicide on October 22. We have an older son, Peter, and the three of us have looked for positive ways to remember Benjamin and to promote ideas that Benjamin would support or enjoy. When Mary, one of my college friends, told me about Little Free Library, I immediately thought, *I want to have a Little Free Library in Benjamin's name.* He was a great reader, and he would have loved the concept of a free library.

We thought long and hard about where the Library should be and eventually settled on Freedom Park in Prescott at the Great River Road Visitor Center. We thought that would be the ideal location since it combines the beauty of nature and a gathering place for people and community events. We love the name "Freedom," and the setting is breathtaking, overlooking the confluence of the Mississippi and St. Croix Rivers.

What meaningful or serendipitous interactions have happened because of your Little Free Library?

After we obtained permission to place the Little Free Library in Freedom Park, we arranged to meet Todd Bol and his wife Susan to install the Library. It was a beautiful, sunny afternoon, and we enjoyed talking with Todd and Susan while erecting the Library with its special nameplate—"Benjamin's Books." After placing the first batch of books into the Library, we strolled off toward our cars to talk some more. Within five minutes, a young boy rode his bicycle up to the Little Free Library, opened the door, and began looking through the books. It was perfect; just what we wanted. It was as if a younger Benjamin had been led to this new resource for reading and sharing books.

As Library stewards, we regularly stop by the Library to restock or rearrange the books. One evening we went to the Little Free Library after dinner to put new stain on the Library walls before winter arrived. As we worked, a husband and wife, Tinka and Otto, approached the Library with books in their hands to share with others. We said we were Benjamin's parents, and they asked us about him. After hearing about Benjamin and why we wanted a Library at Freedom Park, they shared with us that they had also lost two children to untimely and tragic deaths. The four of us stood at the Library and sobbed, sharing our heartache for children no longer with us. Tinka and Otto told us how much they enjoy bringing their grandchildren to the Benjamin's Books LFL and how excited their grandchildren are to discover the new books waiting for them. Now Tinka and Helen have met for walks and talks and even attend a yoga class together. We have each found a new friend who understands what this Little Library means to grieving parents and to adventuresome grandchildren and grandparents.

What books are in your Little Free Library right now?

We generally have many different genres—adult, children's, and some nonfiction titles. Sometimes we put other materials in the Library such as videos, games, and our special Benjamin coins. [Tokens imprinted with the message "Light for Your Path."] I also leave bookmarks, stickers, or other little items for the next visitor to find and take with them.

We really enjoy reading handwritten comments or notes that some people leave on the inside cover of books that are left—a short personal message for the next person who takes that book.

How has the Library had an impact on you and your community?

We have received very positive feedback about the "Benjamin's Books" Little Library. The board members and staff of the Great River Road Learning Center tell us the Library is a great addition to the park. People come to Freedom Park for a variety of events and reasons, and it is common to see families or children opening the door to peek inside. Many books in the Library turn over quickly, and we often find new books that have been left by others.

The Little Free Library has been a cathartic experience for us. We are so happy to remember our son in this unique way while promoting the sharing and reading of good books, a concept that Benjamin would love and fully support.

BOOKS FOR AFRICA

Ghana, Nigeria, and other African countries

Charter Number: Multiple

Through its Good Global Neighbors program, Little Free Library brings Libraries and books where they're needed, anywhere in the world. Now, they've teamed with Books for Africa—an organization that has delivered more than 30 million books to forty-nine different countries since 1988—to bring two thousand Little Libraries to the African continent.

The first shipment of one-of-a-kind Libraries—painted in bright colors and patterns to celebrate Africa—traveled to Ghana in West Africa. Partners in Tanzania, Nigeria, Ethiopia, Gambia, South Africa, and other countries will receive them as well.

Many of the people who live in the villages that will receive Little Free Libraries have never had the opportunity to own, or even hold, a book. Having free books available to everyone in the community is a great benefit. "There's always so much excitement when we visit and the books have been received," says Patrick Plonski, executive director of Books for Africa. "There's a party, and there's dancing, and politicians will come and make speeches. They make a big deal out of books."

Atlases and current encyclopedias are some of the most useful types of books that Books for Africa sends overseas, but textbooks, fiction, children's books, and everything in between are also valued. "It's really about variety and getting the right books to the right people," Plonski says.

Little Free Library and Books for Africa will petition businesses, organizations, and individuals to raise the $1,000 needed to design, build, and ship each Library—which will come with $1,000 worth of books. Rotary International, another friend to Little Free Library, will assist with distribution and installation of the Libraries.

Local residents are eager for Little Free Libraries to arrive in their areas. "Reading will help me travel the world without getting in an airplane," says Benjamin, a student in Kisumu, Karateng-Kenya. Visit littlefreelibrary.org to find out how you can help sponsor a Little Free Library that will make a difference to an entire village.

MARGRET ALDRICH

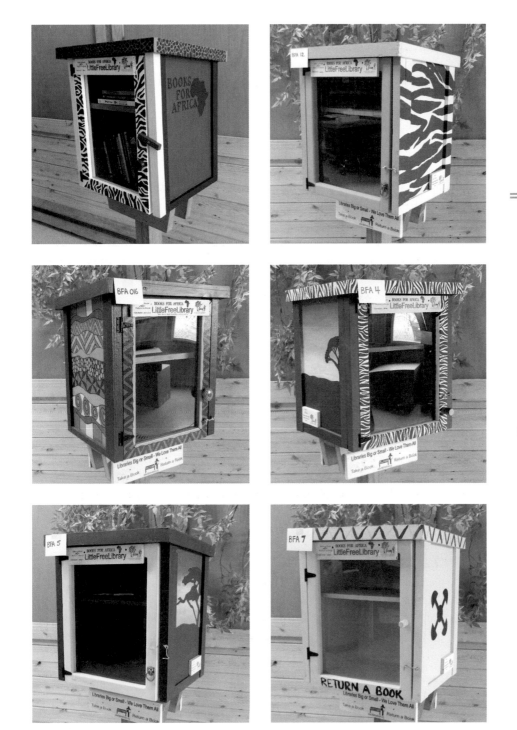

"There's a party, and there's dancing, and politicians will come and make speeches. They make a big deal out of books."

—PATRICK PLONSKI

TARIQ SALEEM MARWAT

Lakki Marwat, Khyber Pakhtunkhwa, Pakistan

Charter Number: 2967 and others

Dr. Tariq Saleem Marwat is a Little Free Library pioneer in Pakistan. He had always loaned books from his personal collection to friends and family; then, in 1997, he decided to loan books out in a different way.

"I hit upon an idea to install a mailbox and would put new arrivals in it," he says. "My friends would come and read the books. Some would take them and later return them back—they would leave a note in the notebook that they were taking that particular book. When I saw the Little Free Library website, I loved the idea and contacted them."

So far, Marwat has built seven Little Free Libraries in his home country. Most of the books that fill these Little Libraries are thick hardcovers in local dialects, but some English-language books—such as the Kitty Kelley's biography of Oprah Winfrey or a Scooby-Doo adventure—have also shown up.

Marwat intends to build thirteen more Little Libraries in Pakistan. For his efforts, Little Free Library cofounders Todd Bol and Rick Brooks awarded him

MARGRET ALDRICH

the first Golden Neighbor Literacy Award, which reads, "For being an excellent example of positive change by creating better access to books and stronger communities in Pakistan and by serving as an example for all of Asia."

MARIA GALLEGOS

Dillon, Montana, USA

Charter Number: 5581

Maria Gallegos built her Little Free Library as a thank-you to the residents of her small town of Dillon, Montana, who had been enormously supportive when she moved to Dillon and bought what she calls "the town's biggest little dumpsite of a house." The yard was a tangle of weeds, and the house itself—part of which was a tiny log cabin built in the 1800s—had been neglected for a decade and was in clear need of renovation.

Neighbors regularly stopped by to watch the progress and help where they could. "So many people had a story to share about my house and its history," Maria says. "By the time I fought off the weeds to make room for a small garden in the far corner of my backyard, I felt it was time to show my appreciation to a community that had embraced me and my immense undertaking."

Maria's schoolhouse-style Little Free Library is painted hot-chili red with a silver-plated bell on top. And while she loves to read, the Library isn't just about books. "For such a small library, it has an enormously large heart, Gallegos says. "Like most meeting places, my minuscule Library is a wonderful gathering and giving place. It brings out the absolute best in people within our small, close-knit community."

Neighbors have been generous in many ways, from dropping off books to donating building materials to other, more creative kindnesses. A coworker built a bench from hewn logs to sit alongside the Little Library. Salesclerks at the local secondhand store invited Maria to take boxes of books at no charge, whenever the LFL needed them. The neighborhood's newspaper carriers (a husband-and-wife team) delivered a free copy of the local paper to the Library every morning. And another Good Samaritan pulled his car up to the Library, thanked Maria for building it, and gave her a hundred-dollar bill. "I was speechless," Maria says. "He told me the money was to help buy whatever materials I might need to help fix up the area. I hugged him through the open window of his car!"

Beyond her immediate community, Gallegos has also connected to the greater community of Little Free Library stewards, and when she travels, she makes sure to stop and visit them. "I traveled to North Carolina this past October and looked up the only Little Free Library in Asheville, to trade out a book and meet the stewards," she says. "They had us in for tea, and we swapped Library stories." Maria has also visited stewards in Portland, Oregon, and Helena, Montana.

"It is obvious that the goodwill among people knows absolutely no bounds or borders," Maria says, "and I am so very pleased to be a part of such a magical movement. My Little Free Library is a gift that I gave to my community, and it continues to give amazing gifts back to me."

ORGANIZING A COMMUNITY BUILD DAY

Working with others to build and install Little Free Libraries is a wonderful way to accomplish more—and have more fun—in less time. Follow these steps to get your project started.

Define your goal
Why do you want to bring Little Free Libraries to your community? Where will they be placed? Who will benefit from them? Communicating your intentions and passion for the project will help you get people on board.

Find volunteers
A Little Free Library build day is a great one-day project for friends and family, neighborhood associations, and other groups. Local schools can rally parents, teachers, and students to help. Clubs like Rotary, Lions, Kiwanis, and Jaycees are often looking for a service project, as are groups such as Girl Scouts, Boy Scouts, and 4-H. Small, midsize, and large companies are also good candidates for a Little Free Library build day, and often treat it as a team-building opportunity.

For some groups, build days can be organized around a special platform. The band Foster the People, for example, used their Do Good campaign and Foster the Future initiative to wrangle build-day volunteers online and were able to build twelve Little Free Libraries in less than five hours.

Gather materials

Do you want to build and decorate only one Little Free Library? Four? Twenty? Pick a number that is attainable for the number of volunteers you'll have on hand. Then decide if you want to build from scratch or order pre-cut (or even prepainted) kits from the Little Free Library organization to easily assemble. Raise funds from the groups you're working with, the wider community, or through crowdsourcing sites like Kickstarter. Collect books from community members. Ask local lumberyards and hardware stores to donate materials. See "Funding Your Library" on page 48 for more ideas.

Request charter numbers and signs

By registering your Libraries at littlefreelibrary.org beforehand, you'll have the official signage ready to attach to the Libraries during the build day. Each registration costs less than forty dollars and should be covered by the funds that you raise for the project or from the recipient of the Little Library.

Alert the media

Local newspapers, television stations, and bloggers may be interested in seeing what you're up to—especially if it's a larger project. Write up a press release with date, time, and other pertinent information, and send it out to major outlets.

Get it done—and have a good time

Give everyone at the build day a job. Skilled craftspeople can cut and assemble the Little Free Library structures. Creative types can plan and execute the Libraries' decoration. Teens and kids can get in on the painting and serve as event photographers. Volunteers with large vehicles can transport and install the Little Free Libraries. Book lovers can stock the Libraries with titles for young and adult readers. And others can help make it a party, providing snacks, beverages, and music for the event.

Follow up

Send thank-you notes to volunteers via e-mail, social media, or post. Keep in touch with the recipients of your Little Free Libraries, and stop by often to see if they need help maintaining or restocking their shelves.

MORE THAN BOOKS

Every now and then, delight Little Free Library visitors with small surprises that aren't books. During the month of December, for example, I stock my Library with a jar full of red-and-white-striped candy canes. Here are a few other fun ideas:

■ Plant a container garden of herbs and cherry tomatoes next to your Little Free Library, and encourage patrons to pick some to take home. Or plant flowers suitable for cutting next to your Library, so visitors can make a bouquet. Tie a small pair of scissors to the side of the Library for easy cuts.

■ Keep the neighborhood kids coming back with a Little Free Treasure Chest: leave a small box in your Library for exchanging all those tiny plastic toys, stickers, tattoos, and special rocks that children invariably collect.

■ Place a wishbox in your Little Library. Patrons can leave a note asking for help or kind thoughts, whether they are going through an illness, have lost a loved one, or just need a helping hand in the yard. Other visitors can read the notes and find out where they can be of service.

■ Leave a few dog biscuits in your Little Free Library and a dish full of water beside it for four-legged visitors. That way, their owners aren't the only ones who walk away with a treat.

■ One weekend a month, put a "free box" next to your Library for whatever items your neighbors want to trade, like winter mittens, records, movies, and coffee mugs.

■ Choose your favorite Little Free Library in your neighborhood. Make a thank-you card telling the steward why you love their Library, and have as many people sign it as possible. Leave it in the Little Library with a pen so visitors can leave their well-wishes, too.

KIMBERLY AND JAMES DAUGHERTY

Topeka, Kansas, USA

Charter Number: Multiple

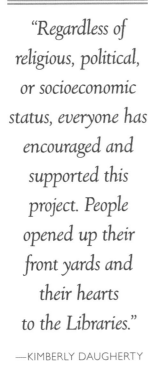

"Regardless of religious, political, or socioeconomic status, everyone has encouraged and supported this project. People opened up their front yards and their hearts to the Libraries."

—KIMBERLY DAUGHERTY

When Kimberly and James Daugherty erected the first Little Free Library in Topeka in their front yard, they didn't know it would spark a local movement. The Library caught the attention of Sheyvette Dinkens, executive director of Women Empowerment, Inc., an organization that provides resources to at-risk girls. Sheyvette contacted Kimberly to talk about bringing more Little Libraries to the area, explaining that they could really make a difference to the teenage girls in her program.

"Sheyvette said as the girls in her program read more books, they became more confident about education, college, and career options. And she felt that if we could bring more Little Free Libraries to Topeka neighborhoods, we would empower more children," Kimberly says. "I agreed and committed my husband to building twenty Little Free Libraries to be dispersed around the city."

The twenty Little Libraries went up, and the feel-good response came pouring in. "We heard stories of kids sitting in front yards reading. We heard of folks who lived next door to one another for five years having a conversation for the first time. I once observed a neighbor talk with a Library steward about a recent break-in and discuss keeping an eye on each other's homes. I watched the city I love become more about neighbors again. I watched people slow down and take a minute to speak to one another instead of rushing in and out of their homes. Yet, this was still just the beginning for us and our project."

Twenty *more* Little Libraries were built, and this time it was a team effort: the Daughertys partnered with the local Blue Cross Blue Shield branch to get books about good health habits in English and Spanish; a local roofing company provided shingles; Casey's General Store donated plexiglass, the most expensive material for the Libraries; and Boy Scout and Girl Scout troops included Little Free Libraries in their service projects. "We even hosted a build day where teens on probation came out and helped us build seventeen Libraries. It was really cool to see kids go from looking put out and bored to laughing, talking about their favorite books, and begging to come back to help again," Kimberly says.

To date, thirty-two of the finished Little Free Libraries have been installed around Topeka, many in heavily trafficked areas such as the children's museum, the community resource center, and the Equality House—the brightly painted

"Rainbow House" that stands across the street from Westboro Baptist Church headquarters, in peaceful support of the LGBTQ community.

"On a community level, our experience with Little Free Library has been incredible," Kimberly says. "Regardless of religious, political, or socioeconomic status, everyone has encouraged and supported this project. People opened up their front yards and their hearts to the Libraries."

MARGRET ALDRICH

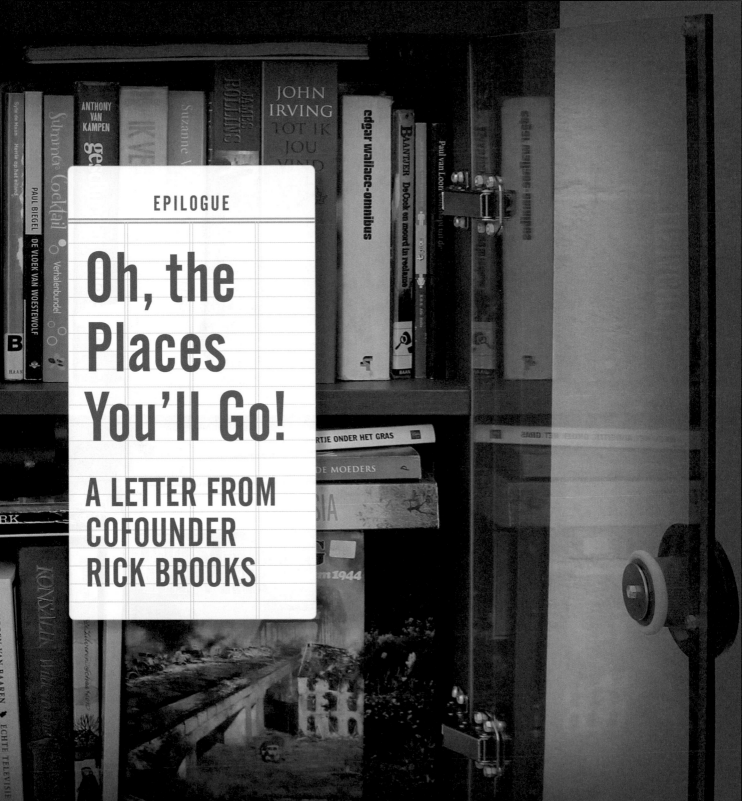

Oh, the Places You'll Go!

A LETTER FROM COFOUNDER RICK BROOKS

"A good book

has no ending."

—R. D. CUMMING

OH, THE PLACES YOU'LL GO!
A LETTER FROM COFOUNDER RICK BROOKS

Thank you, Dr. Seuss. One of my fantasies comes from you. It is to have *National Geographic* send someone on a round-the-word expedition to discover the most exotic locations for Little Free Libraries. We've seen snapshots of them in the wilds of Montana and Los Angeles, and at the foot of a mountain in Sri Lanka. Even downtown Manhattan can claim a network of Little Libraries. They've been declared "cool" by the trendsetters of popular culture. Anchorage, Bangalore and Hanoi have them!

So . . . where might these mighty little boxes of joy and wonder and education and mystery and poetry take us in 2015 and beyond? We can imagine and guess, but we really want to know.

Judging from the daily barrage of e-mails and photographs sent with new Little Library registrations, Dr. Seuss himself, if he were still alive, would love the journey. Why? Because the motivations behind Little Free Libraries are so diverse . . . and so fundamentally similar.

Somewhere in the political turmoil of countries ranging from Ukraine to the United States, Little Free Libraries may be part of the inspiration and support for a resurgence of civil society. We hope so. A single Little Library in a refugee camp in Uganda serves thousands of displaced children and adults. In Sierra

Leone, Kenya, and the Congo, each tiny outpost for books is like a seed to help satisfy the hunger for knowledge and belonging. The same goes for Mediapolis, Iowa, where a legacy Library honors small-town doctors over the past century. Tiny towns and urban neighborhoods across the United States are adopting the idea of neighborhood book exchanges. It's hard not to love that.

The stories continue. An international group of readers in Tokyo is building robot Libraries. Geocachers are finding their way to Little Libraries on nearly every continent now, stashing surprises among the volumes of words and pictures. BookCrossing fans are tracking the journeys of their favorite titles.

To me, however, it's not the big numbers and hoopla that matter. Instead, it's the daily scenario of neighbors meeting neighbors from near and far, some in person and others in the pages of books. From the Library in front of my family's house on Mason Street here in Madison, Wisconsin, Garrison Keillor's latest novel took wing within one day. Volume 20 of a series by Victor Hugo from the 1890s and the 1920 edition of the Girl Scout manual took a little longer. I suspect the person who got them wasn't quite sure she could believe they were free for the taking.

Having personally installed several hundred of these little guys gives Todd and me an unfair advantage over just about anyone else in the Little Free

Library world. We get to meet many of the stewards face to face. In the beginning, people would drive or walk by and wonder what we were doing. Then, when they had read about Little Free Libraries or seen us on TV, they would honk. High school kids would high five us, and moms started to hug us. Our own mothers might have wondered what was responsible for such transformations in their sons.

We weren't giving out money or doing anything particularly saintly. But something was going on that was definitely bigger than we were, and the Little Free Library stewards, then and now, embodied that spirit.

In retrospect, it wasn't just the books or their cute containers. It was the idea that people could trust each other enough to exchange part of themselves for the greater good.

According to a Wisconsin Public Television feature, Madison resident James Roberts has established a yearly tradition of trying to ride his bicycle to every Little Library in town. In his moments of cinematic stardom, James said and did pretty much everything right—he took a journey of discovery from neighborhood to neighborhood, had fun, and discovered a cornucopia of reading material. He whistled while he pedaled. We can see his eyebrows raised at both the mystery and delight. Cool!

All of these stories are—what's the best metaphor?—the icing on the cake, the sizzle on the steak, and the cat's pajamas. Or as our younger aficionados might say in an IM or a tweet, a totally epic display of awesomeness. Each incarnation of the original one-room schoolhouse model offers a more exciting turn.

If you visit the online photos on Flickr and Pinterest, you'll know what we mean. For me, the most gratifying rewards are scenes like these—a group of elementary school kids sitting under a tree listening to a fourth grader read aloud; or dog walkers stopping to open the door of the Little Library and finding, to their amazement, the book they had been seeking for years.

In late spring and summer, my wife and I sit on our front porch for dinner and wait for such events to happen. It doesn't take long. The passing parade on our block reminds me of Norman Rockwell and Beverly Cleary. We wouldn't be surprised to see Beezus and Ramona in person, because our Little Library patrons include as many kids as grownups.

Makes me think of *The Biggest Bear, Make Way for Ducklings,* and, yes, Albert Camus, not to mention Mark Twain. Those books and authors deserve more than a lifetime of collecting dust, and it is our pleasure to share them. I donated my favorite book of all time, Alan Paton's *Cry, the Beloved Country,* to a Little Free Library in Chicago, for example, in the hope that someone else could discover what I did when I read it in 1958. My mother had given it to me for my tenth

birthday so that I could learn what apartheid was. At the time, I was unaware that anyone could write the way Paton did; that he could invent a way of storytelling that would change my life.

These days, my bed often looks like the squeeze-box that autistic activist Temple Grandin uses to calm herself down. I am surrounded by books. They keep me warm. They give me comfort.

For years, books have been the currency of interpersonal revelation, like treasure chests of vicarious experience. Paragraph by paragraph, chapter by chapter, they have taken me far beyond the confines of my own life. Something of mine, *part of me* and what I value, can now be freed from untouched decades on our family bookshelves.

That is our gift. Or not. Our hope, which may not be such a dream after all, is that somehow, bringing quality books into new hands, hearts, and minds can generate more readers, better students, and more engaged citizens.

Are we dreaming? Are the police stations in St. Louis and Los Angeles that have embraced Little Free Libraries just fooling themselves and indulging in simplistic formulas for crime prevention? Should we worry that the popularity of Little *Free* Libraries might tempt taxpayers to balk at supporting public libraries?

MARGRET ALDRICH

Truth is, we don't know. But we choose to believe in the goodness of it all. We didn't know when Little Free Library was in its infancy that it would also offer paths of such little resistance to so many different dreamers and doers. Take these, for instance:

- Scouts and 4-H club members, husbands, and craftsmen retirees who had absolutely no idea what they might build next.
- Gardeners, lovers of heritage seeds, and fans of ethnic recipes who want to share what they love.
- New authors and poets whose work might never have made it past the pile of literary agents' incoming mail.
- Lifetime book hoarders who finally can be reassured that their efforts have not been in vain.
- Memory makers. Treasure hunters. With every new Little Free Library, the chances of serendipitous discovery increase.

Then there's Maya Stein and Amy Tingle's tandem bike ride 1,400 miles from Colorado to southern Wisconsin, writing poetry and building Little Free Libraries along the way. Knitters whose yarn bombs kept their Little Libraries warm in the winter, carpenter/humorists who built Libraries to look like a giant rooster, the State Capitol of Iowa, and the TARDIS, Dr. Who's personal time machine.

Have you seen any of those? When you hear that the only future of public libraries is digital, or that books are going the way of the brontosaurus, you can take comfort in such whimsy and devotion. Maybe someone who discovers a book in Timbuktu or the South Pole will join you. If that book found its way from one of our neighbors' Little Free Libraries, we will be rewarded beyond our wildest hopes.

—Rick Brooks

CONNECT WITH LITTLE FREE LIBRARY

On the web:
littlefreelibrary.org

World Map:
littlefreelibrary.org/ourmap

Facebook:
facebook.com/LittleFreeLibrary

Twitter:
twitter.com/LtlFreeLibrary

Pinterest:
pinterest.com/ltlfreelibrary

Flickr:
flickr.com/photos/68010601@N03

Instagram:
instagram.com/littlefreelibrary

Neighborhood Library Builders Guild:
facebook.com/pages/Neighborhood-Library-Builders-Guild

NYC PEN Festival LFL:
archleague.org/2013/07/little-free-library-nyc-design-guidelines-
and-installation-instructions

CONSTRUCTION PLANS

Are you ready to build your own Library? On the next few pages you will find complete instructions for a basic model you can make in your garage or basement. This example has been designed with the amateur woodworker in mind. Construction requires only basic tools. Even the plywood sheeting (you will need three 2' x 4' pieces) is small enough to be transported from the lumberyard in a compact car.

You will find detailed instructions showing how to layout the parts on your plywood, tips for sawing the pieces to size, and step-by-step procedures for nailing and gluing the project together.

After completing the basic construction, we invite you to use your imagination to further dress up your library. For example, you might add a steeple and paint the project white to create a church. A simple bell tower and a coat of red paint will turn it into a school house. Or by adding just the right decorations, you could turn it into a gingerbread house.

Whatever route you take, you will find that building your own Little Free Library will be a valuable experience.

EDITOR'S NOTE: The plans for this version of the Little Free Library were designed by Paul Meisel of Mound, Minnesota, and are reproduced with permission. You can purchase additional copies of this plan (order plan #W3651), windows for the church steeple (part #8607), 1" bells (part #9262), 2-1/2" bells (part #9263), as well as the hinges and other hardware specified with asterisks in the Bill of Materials from Meisel Hardware Specialties, P. O. Box 70, Mound, MN 55364, (800) 441-9870, www.meiselwoodhobby.com. The Library and accessories pictured below were constructed by American Workshop, www.americanworkshop.com.

LITTLE FREE LIBRARY CONSTRUCTION PLANS | PAGE #1

Bill of Materials

QTY.	PART	SIZE OF MATERIAL
2	Front & Rear	7/16" x 21" x 22"
2	Left & Right Side	7/16" x 13" x 13-1/8"
1	Bottom	7/16" x 13-1/8" x 20-1/8" (Not Drawn)
2	Left & Right Roof	7/16" x 13-3/16" x 17-3/4"
2	Front & Back Bottom Support	7/16" x 1-1/2" x 17-1/8" (Not Drawn)
2	Left & Right Bottom Support	7/16" x 1-1/2" x 13-1/8" (Not Drawn)
1	Post Mount	7/16" x 7" x 7-1/2" (Not Drawn)
1	Door	7/16" x14-1/2" x 18-3/4"
2	Window Frame Sides	7/16" x 3/4" x 10-7/8"
2	Window Frame Top & Bottom	7/16" x 3/4" x 15-1/8"
4	Front & Back Fascia	7/16" x 1" x 13-7/8"
2	Left & Right Fascia	7/16" x 1-1/16" x 17-3/4"
4	Front & Back Corner Trim	7/16" x 1-1/2" x 16-9/16"
4	Left & Right Corner Trim	7/16" x 1" x 15-15/16"
1 pair	Hinge, "Hammer Finish" Colonial*	2-9/16" (#8143)
1	Hook and Eye*	1-1/2" (#1286)
1	Knob, Black*	1-1/8" Dia. (#1734)
1	Acrylic Sheet	1/8" x 10" x 14-1/4"

* Available from Meisel Hardware Specialties. To request a catalog, write to Meisel Hardware Specialties, P. O. Box 70, Mound, MN 55364-0070, PH 1-800-441-9870. www.meiselwoodhobby.com.

Copyright and "Permission to Use" Statement

LITTLE FREE LIBRARY CONSTRUCTION PLANS | PAGE #2

MARGRET ALDRICH

Plan of Procedure

This project is constructed from plywood. Since plywood thickness varies (i.e., 1/2" plywood often measures closer to 7/16" in actual thickness) this plan is designed to use 7/16" thick plywood. You can use full 1/2" thick plywood (if available) but some very minor changes will need to be made such as cutting the length of the Bottom and Front & Back Bottom Supports 1/8" smaller than called out.

The entire project can be made from three pieces of 2' x 4' plywood. The cutting diagram shows one way to lay out the parts.

The purpose of the Post Mount piece is to reinforce the bottom of the project for attaching a mailbox type bracket which will slide onto a 4" x 4" wood post for mounting the project outdoors. This mounting technique eliminates the need for the 45-degree brace described on page 243. This piece will not be needed of you will be placing the project on a table or counter top inside a building.

Drawings are neither provided nor needed for the Bottom, the Post Mount, or the Front, Back, and Left & Right Bottom Supports. These are all simple rectangular shaped pieces. Cut them to the width and length called for in the Bill of Materials.

Begin by cutting all the parts as described below. Then assemble the project according to the Final Assembly Instructions and as shown in the exploded Assembly Drawing.

FRONT & BACK: Layout and cut to size. Cut the opening in the Front piece only. (One of each piece required.)

LEFT & RIGHT SIDE: Layout and cut to size. Cut the 30-degree bevel. (Two pieces required.)

BOTTOM: Layout and cut to size according to the dimensions given in the Bill of Materials.

LEFT & RIGHT ROOF: Layout and cut to size. Cut the 30-degree bevels. (Two pieces required.)

FRONT & BACK BOTTOM SUPPORT: Layout and cut to size according to the dimensions given in the Bill of Materials. (Two pieces required.)

LEFT & RIGHT BOTTOM SUPPORT: Layout and cut to size according to the dimensions given in the Bill of Materials. (Two pieces required.)

POST MOUNT: Layout and cut to size according to the dimensions given in the Bill of Materials.

DOOR: LAYOUT AND CUT TO SIZE. Cut the four window cutouts (note you could also make one large opening rather than four small openings). Drill the 3/16" diameter hole through.

WINDOW FRAME SIDES, WINDOW FRAME TOP & BOTTOM: Begin by ripping strips of plywood 3/4" wide. Cut a 1/8" deep by 3/8" wide rabbet along one edge of these strips. From these strips cut the Top, Bottom, and two Side Window Frame pieces to length with a 45-degree miter at each end. Important—note direction of miter (rabbets must be on the inside of the frame pieces when assembled). (One Top, one Bottom, and two Side pieces required.)

FRONT & BACK FASCIA: Layout and cut to size. Cut the 30-degree bevel as shown. (Two pieces required.)

LEFT & RIGHT FASCIA: Layout and cut to size. Cut the 30-degree bevel as shown. (Two pieces required.)

FRONT & BACK CORNER TRIM: Layout and cut to size. Cut the 30 degree angle. (Two Pieces Required)

LITTLE FREE LIBRARY CONSTRUCTION PLANS | PAGE #3

LEFT & RIGHT CORNER TRIM: Layout and cut to size. Cut the 30-degree angle. (Two pieces required.)

WINDOW: Cut a piece of 1/8" Acrylic plastic to the size called out in the Bill of Materials.

FINAL ASSEMBLY:

STEP 1: Glue and nail the Front & Back and Left & Right Bottom Support Pieces to the underside of the Bottom piece. Glue and nail the Post Mount piece, centered under the Bottom piece. Glue and nail the Side pieces to the Bottom assembly, flush to the bottom edge. Glue and nail the Front and Back pieces to the Sides and Bottom assembly.

STEP 2: Glue and nail the Roof pieces (with a 2-1/2" overhang on the front) to the Front, Back, and Side pieces. Glue and nail the Left and Right Fascia pieces to the Roof. Glue and nail the Front and Back Fascia pieces to the Roof. Glue and nail the Left and Right Corner Trim pieces in place. Glue and nail the Front and Back Corner Trim pieces in place.

Now is a good time to paint the project. Use a quality acrylic latex house primer and paint in the colors of your choice.

STEP 3: Center the Acrylic Sheet over the cutout on the inside of the Door. The Acrylic Sheet is attached using the Window Frame Side, Top, and Bottom pieces. Drill holes and screw (no glue) these pieces in place. Attach the Hinges approximately 2" from the top and bottom of the Door. Cut the Knob Screw to length and attach the Knob where shown. Attach the Screen Door Hook at the midway point of the Door.

If placing your project on a 4" x 4" wood post, you may wish to purchase a bracket such as the type used for mounting mailboxes. For indoor use, simply place the project on a shelf or countertop.

SAFETY PRECAUTIONS

The designer, copyright holder, draftsperson, printer, distributor, and editor do not assume responsibility for injury incurred by persons who perform the cutting, drilling, or other machining, sanding, or finishing operations necessary to build this project, nor do they assume responsibility for costs of materials spoiled due to errors caused by incorrect measurements, persons misreading dimensions, etc.

This project plan is provided with the understanding that persons building the project described do not attempt any cutting, drilling, machining, sanding, or finishing operation which they do not have the ability to perform safely. Use and dispose of finishing materials, adhesives, solvents, and other chemicals according to EPA regulations and OSHA and other appropriate regulatory agencies. Keep plans, woodworking tools, finishes, and adhesives out of the reach of children.

When building any woodworking project, especially projects which may be used by children, use caution that there are no rough or sharp edges or loose parts which could cause injury. Homemade woodworking projects are not recommended for children under three years of age.

LITTLE FREE LIBRARY CONSTRUCTION PLANS | PAGE #4

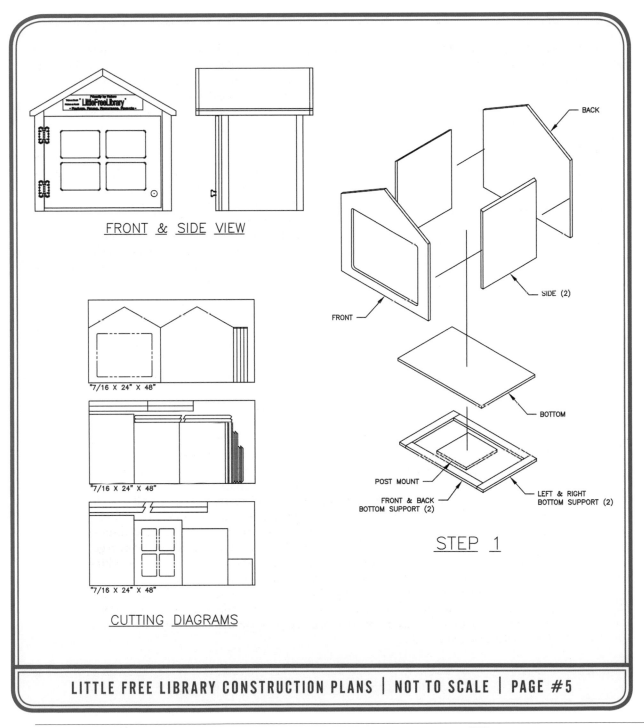

FRONT & SIDE VIEW

BACK

SIDE (2)

FRONT

BOTTOM

POST MOUNT

FRONT & BACK
BOTTOM SUPPORT (2)

LEFT & RIGHT
BOTTOM SUPPORT (2)

STEP 1

"7/16 X 24" X 48"

"7/16 X 24" X 48"

"7/16 X 24" X 48"

CUTTING DIAGRAMS

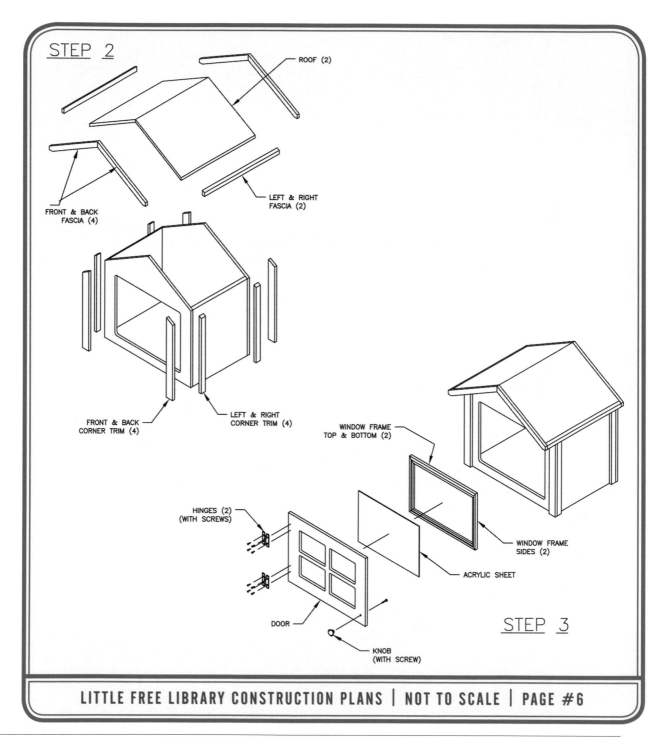

STEP 2

ROOF (2)

FRONT & BACK
FASCIA (4)

LEFT & RIGHT
FASCIA (2)

FRONT & BACK
CORNER TRIM (4)

LEFT & RIGHT
CORNER TRIM (4)

WINDOW FRAME
TOP & BOTTOM (2)

WINDOW FRAME
SIDES (2)

HINGES (2)
(WITH SCREWS)

ACRYLIC SHEET

DOOR

STEP 3

KNOB
(WITH SCREW)

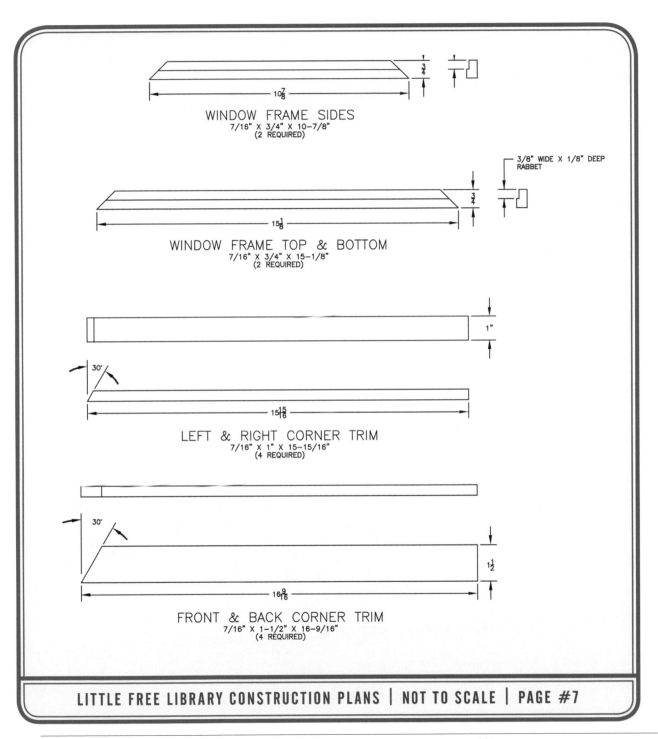

WINDOW FRAME SIDES
7/16" X 3/4" X 10-7/8"
(2 REQUIRED)

WINDOW FRAME TOP & BOTTOM
7/16" X 3/4" X 15-1/8"
(2 REQUIRED)

3/8" WIDE X 1/8" DEEP RABBET

LEFT & RIGHT CORNER TRIM
7/16" X 1" X 15-15/16"
(4 REQUIRED)

FRONT & BACK CORNER TRIM
7/16" X 1-1/2" X 16-9/16"
(4 REQUIRED)

LITTLE FREE LIBRARY CONSTRUCTION PLANS | NOT TO SCALE | PAGE #7

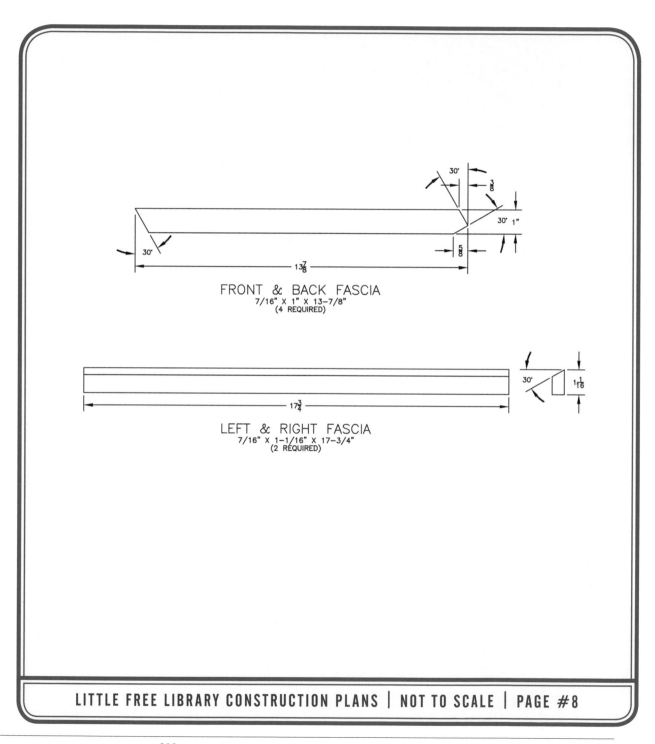

FRONT & BACK FASCIA
7/16" X 1" X 13–7/8"
(4 REQUIRED)

LEFT & RIGHT FASCIA
7/16" X 1–1/16" X 17–3/4"
(2 REQUIRED)

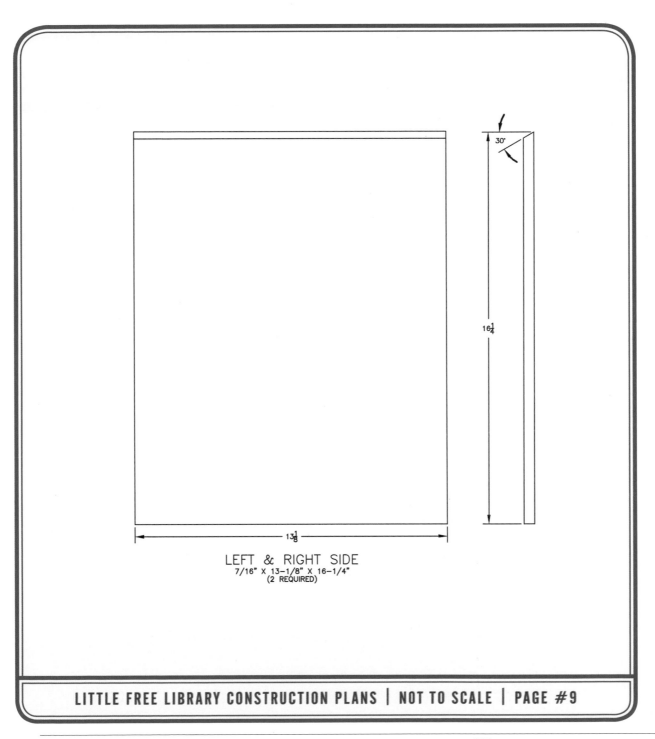

LEFT & RIGHT SIDE
7/16" X 13-1/8" X 16-1/4"
(2 REQUIRED)

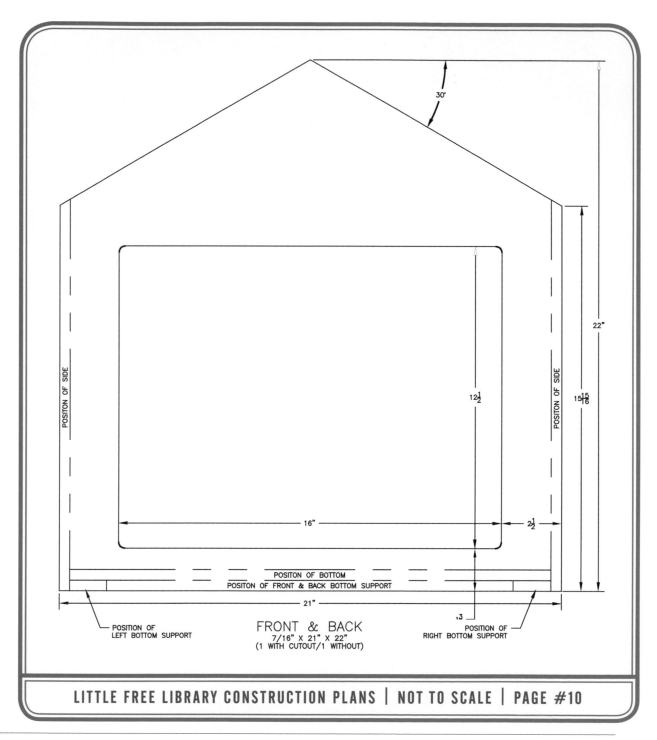

30°

22"

15 15/16

12 1/2

16"

2 1/2

POSITON OF SIDE

POSITON OF SIDE

POSITON OF BOTTOM
POSITON OF FRONT & BACK BOTTOM SUPPORT

21"

.3

POSITION OF
LEFT BOTTOM SUPPORT

POSITION OF
RIGHT BOTTOM SUPPORT

FRONT & BACK
7/16" X 21" X 22"
(1 WITH CUTOUT/1 WITHOUT)

LITTLE FREE LIBRARY CONSTRUCTION PLANS | NOT TO SCALE | PAGE #10

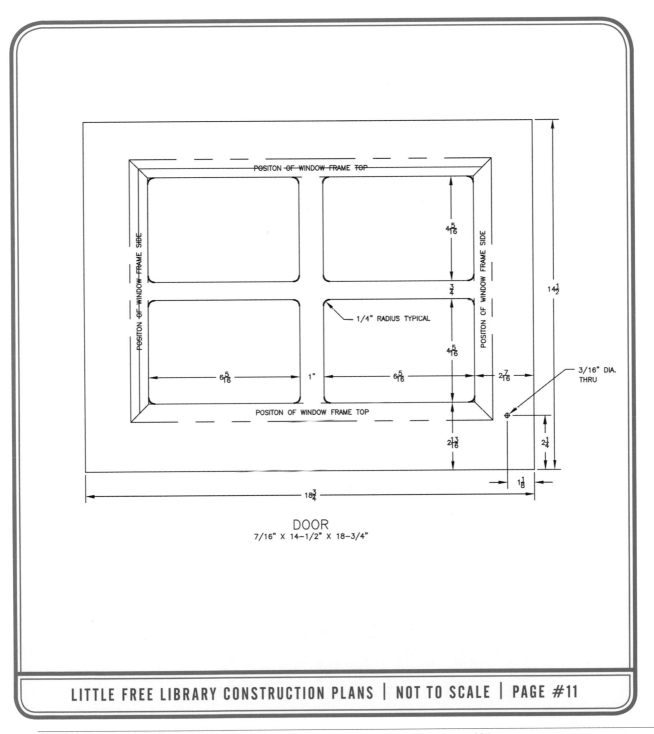

POSITON OF WINDOW FRAME TOP

POSITON OF WINDOW FRAME SIDE

POSITON OF WINDOW FRAME SIDE

1/4" RADIUS TYPICAL

$6\frac{5}{16}$

1"

$6\frac{5}{16}$

$4\frac{5}{16}$

$\frac{3}{4}$

$4\frac{5}{16}$

$2\frac{7}{16}$

POSITON OF WINDOW FRAME TOP

$2\frac{13}{16}$

$14\frac{1}{2}$

3/16" DIA. THRU

$2\frac{1}{4}$

$1\frac{1}{8}$

$18\frac{3}{4}$

DOOR
7/16" X 14–1/2" X 18–3/4"

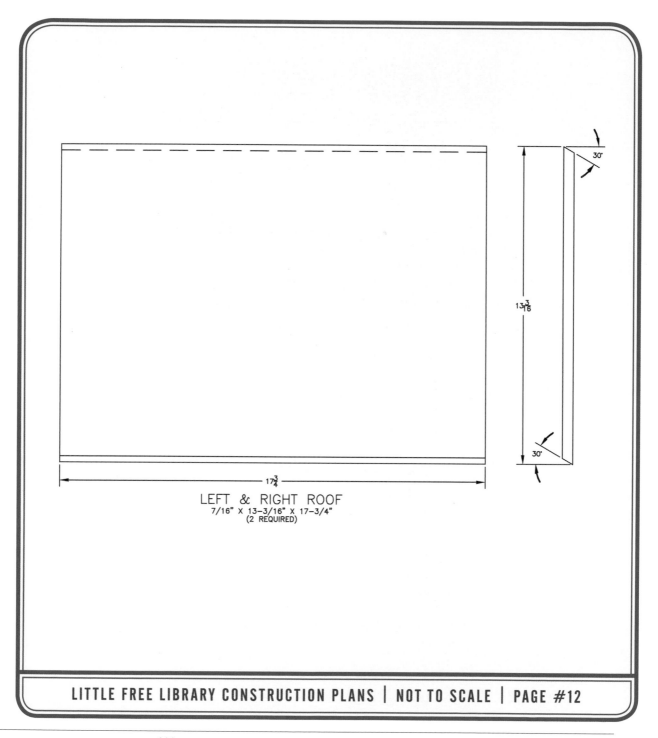

LEFT & RIGHT ROOF
7/16" X 13-3/16" X 17-3/4"
(2 REQUIRED)

The bottom and side pieces have been cut to size.

To ensure a straight cut, clamp a scrap wood strip to guide the saw.

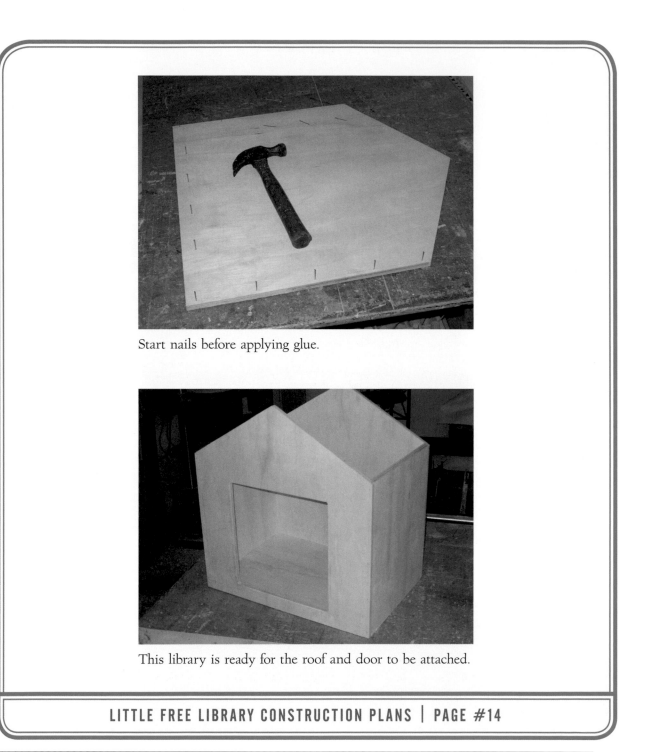

Start nails before applying glue.

This library is ready for the roof and door to be attached.

MARGRET ALDRICH

TIPS FOR BUILDERS

by Todd Bol, Creator, Executive Director, and First Steward of Little Free Library

I would like to communicate to you as a professional woodworker and experienced carpenter, but I cannot. I am just a hobbyist who tinkers on his deck with a portable table saw. It would probably take me sixty hours to do what a competent carpenter could do in ten hours, and my work wouldn't be as perfect. So I mention my simple skill set as encouragement to anyone with the desire and elementary woodworking experience to tackle the rewarding task of building a Little Free Library.

Having built thirty or forty Libraries and renovated or repaired at least one hundred built by others at the time I wrote these words, I hope that Do-It-Yourself hobbyists and professional carpenters will find these tips helpful.

In the Beginning: Some Basic Principles

Our first Little Libraries were roughly twenty inches wide by fifteen inches deep by eighteen inches high, mounted on a sturdy post or secure foundation. Most of them were variations on the idea of a small, one-room building with a gabled roof. Now we're seeing an almost infinite variety of sizes and shapes, including Libraries that can house two or three shelves instead of just one. You most certainly can vary the dimensions and materials as you see fit. But here are some good general principles:

- Use recycled, salvaged, and found materials if you can.
- Use green building techniques whenever possible.
- Build the Library to last. Most Libraries will be outside by a sidewalk, bike path, or walking path, so they will need protection from rain, high and low temperatures, wind, and snow. The shelves should be strong and the box water-tight. The outside walls and top should be weather resistant. If they are not, you may need to have an interior plywood lining.
- Make it safe. Avoid using glass or any other material that may cause harm to curious children or adults. Use plexiglass on the door(s) so that passersby can see the books inside. If you use old wood, be sure it does not have lead paint on it! If you use metal, file off the burrs and rough edges.
- Make sure the signs on your Library are easy to read from five to ten feet away.

- Don't feel obliged to build your Library exactly like the ones you see.
- Always make sure you register each Library so it's in the global network map and benefits from all the promotional and technical support.

Recycle, Repurpose, Reuse

As much as possible, I try to use excess building materials, old wood, and scraps of metal for as many parts of the Little Library as I can. My father passed away recently, and I have included pieces of our family barn, house, old mailbox, and other memorabilia into the Library. I see this as a living legacy, and it makes me smile to see our family living on in the yards and parks of communities across the country.

To date I have used the following:

- recycled wood from a barn destroyed by a tornado
- old garage doors and windows
- smashed mailboxes and old corrugated metal
- discarded deck railings and plastic lattice
- coffee cans, soup cans, and old rulers
- oak barn stalls, dog and doll houses, fencing, and cranberry, milk, and apple crates
- bells, old electrical fuses, and screw driver handles
- discarded materials from building sites (ask first!)

Different Sizes, Different Purposes and Places

In the beginning, a finished Little Library no larger than twenty-two inches wide, fifteen inches deep, and twenty-three inches high was a good size for me. Why? Because it would fit in my station wagon to haul around the country. Plywood was my primary building material. A 4' x 8' sheet of plywood can be difficult to manage. But when you mention that you're building a Little Free Library, friends at lumber yards may even offer to cut the plywood into smaller pieces for you. To get the most from each sheet, I typically ask for pieces 15-7/8" x 23-7/8".

To Keep it Together

I use exterior glue and 1-5/8" to 2-1/2" exterior screws to fasten the plywood panels together. I am careful to use a square to make sure all the sides are at perfect angles. My eyes never seem to see things squarely. The next thing I do is cover the entire inside and outside of the box with an exterior stain or paint, paying special attention to the exposed ends and joints. These are the spots vulnerable to water damage.

By this point I have probably figured out what kind of recycled, repurposed, or excess building material I can use to cover the Library. In the beginning I just used old barn wood, but water leaked inside. Since then I have used the double-wall construction and have not had any problems. This is especially true when I have put a lip of two inches or more above the door to catch rain and keep it from dripping inside the door.

I attach the wood to the plywood base with screws and/or nails, always using exterior glue or liquid nails and being careful that no sharp points stick through the other side of the plywood. This prevents a prickly problem that can occur. I am speaking from experience. We definitely do not want to wound any of our Library patrons with nail points.

Artistic and Architectural Touches

Some general guidelines I learned from the first twenty or more Libraries I have built:

- A ¼" thick, 4" x 5" piece of plywood makes a great decorative window for the side walls. I nail and glue the window and frame it with a ¼" thick piece of contrasting wood trim.
- A 2" wide by 4/5" thick piece of wood makes an excellent door. This is the size used for decking.
- A single door is stronger, more durable, and leaks less than a double door. It's easier to open and it doesn't get chipped or nicked as often.
- Use an exterior hinge or paint an interior hinge with Rust-Oleum.
- I find the greatest creativity is often reflected in the handle. It can be an antique knob, spindle chair back, thimble, tinker toy, or anything else that is easy to use and safe.
- I have used many kinds of exterior stains and paints, and like Sikkens products best and Cabot products second best. Whenever I paint a design on a Library, no matter how elaborate, I always use several layers of exterior clear coat. It's hard to predict how various artistic paints will withstand year-round exposure to the sun and weather. But we know this: Interior paints don't hold up. So be careful. An artist's creation may peel off or fade if it is not done with exterior paints and is not protected by two or three layers of clear coat.

And when your finished, have someone take pictures of you and your friends who helped with the Library and send them to Little Free Library. Follow the instructions on "Get on the Map" on the Little Free Library website. Then try building another Library and giving it away. And then . . .

It's much too rewarding to stop now!

MARGRET ALDRICH

INSTALLATION INSTRUCTIONS
FROM LITTLE FREE LIBRARY

MATERIALS NEEDED

One 8' x 4" x 4" post

One 2' x 2" x 6" piece of wood

Twelve 2-1/2" lag screws

Six 3" exterior lag screws

2-1/2" to 3" lag bolts (optional)

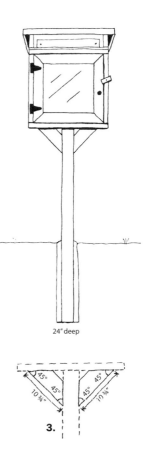

24" deep

1. To start, you will need one 8' x 4" x 4" treated post. Any kind will work, but cedar tone is our favorite.

2. Cut the post to 5' long.

3. With the remaining piece, make side angle braces. Cut each piece 10-3/4" long and cut 45-degree angles on the ends.

4. Cut a platform as wide as the Little Free Library out of the 2' x 2" x 6" piece of wood.

5. Mount the angled braces to the 5' post with 3" exterior lag screws and then attach the platform using six 2-1/2" lag screws. First, predrill a slightly smaller hole to make it easier to install the lag screw. Use lag bolts to enhance the holding power.

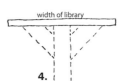

6. Dig a 24" deep hole and install the post. Make sure to use a level and tamp the dirt hard with a shovel to secure the post.

7. Drill six holes through the top of the Little Free Library. The holes need to match up with the post platform. Use the other six 2-1/2" lag screws to attach the platform to the library.

8. You are done! Now take a picture of you and your friends by your Little Free Library and register it via our website at www.littlefreelibrary.org/registeryourlibrary.

9. Build another Little Free Library. People always say that you can't just build one!

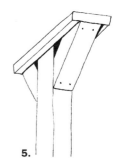

DOOR COUNTER INSTRUCTIONS

Installing a door counter lets you keep track of how many times your Little Free Library is opened and gives you a good idea of how much it's being used. To hook up your Little Free Library with a door counter, follow one of the tutorials below—either a simple or more advanced method.

Easy

For an easy-peasy version, follow this three-step tutorial, courtesy of Viel Catig and her Bicycling Bunny Little Free Library in Chino, California.

1. Get a simple tally counter. These are really cheap at any dollar store. Make sure it is one with a thumb lever.
2. Remove the key ring, and secure the counter using double-sided foam tape about one inch (depending on how thick your door is) inside the Library case. Make sure the reset button is on top so you can access it. Align the edge so the lever gets "pushed" by the door.
3. Test your new door counter by closing and opening your Library door. The numbers on the counter should show how many times your door gets opened. And that's it, you are done! Woohoo!

Advanced

These thorough plans from Jonathan Dickman will provide you with a sturdy door counter to keep a tally of your Little Free Library visitors.

MATERIALS NEEDED

One 15/16" small screw eye with wood-screw threading*

Four 5/8" screws (construction or wood screws would work)

One 1/4" x 1-13/32" extension spring*

Approximately 6 inches of 100-lb fishing line

One mountable mechanical counter with trip arm**

MARGRET ALDRICH

* Different sizes could work as well; what is listed above is what Jonathan has used.

** Multiple versions of mechanical counters are available online by performing a Google search for "5 digit mechanical counter." You may also try your local surplus store.

TOOLS NEDED

Electric drill with a drill-bit extender

Pliers

HOW TO INSTALL THE DOOR COUNTER

1. Tighten the trip arm on the mechanical counter.
2. Place the extension spring on the trip arm.
3. Mount the counter with four screws using the extended-bit drill on the inside corner of the Library. Before mounting, remember to correctly orient your counter so that the trip arm moves forward (the arm may be on top or bottom, depending on how your door opens). The counter should be positioned on the same side as the door hinges. For example, when looking at the door:
   a. If it opens from right to left (hinges on left side), mount the counter on the upper-left corner.
   b. If it opens from left to right (hinges on right side), mount the counter on the upper-right corner.
   c. If it opens from down to up (hinges on top), mount the counter on the top.
4. Use pliers to place the eye screw in the wood of the corner of the Library door just opposite to the counter at the level of the trip arm. Once in place, make sure the door still closes properly before proceeding.
5. Thread the fishing line through the eye screw and tie the ends to form a loop of fishing line.
6. Connect the spring to the loop of fishing line and adjust the fishing line to make the trip arm move. Once you are done adjusting, you are finished!
   a. As long as the loop of fishing line is not too far off, a good way to shorten the fishing line is to make knots in the loop (each knot placed will shorten the loop).
   b. You want the fishing line to be short enough to trip the counter without needing to open the door all the way, but not so short that the trip arm goes into its resting position when the door closes.

Common Problems and What to Do

1. Sometimes the trip arm on the mechanical counter is not in a position that will be functional for the Library. Try changing the position of the arm before mounting the counter by twisting the arm in the opposite direction that it would normally go for counting.

2. If the number on the counter is not going up when you open the door, make sure the fishing line is not too tight or too loose. There is a possibility that it could become too loose over time as the spring stretches out. On the other hand, if the fishing line is too tight, then the trip arm will not go back far enough to achieve its resting position, which is necessary for the counter to detect the next door opening.

Permission to use the door counter tutorial was given by Jonathan Dickman, MD, PhD. This work was completed while Dr. Dickman was a medical student in TRaining In Urban Medicine and Public Health (TRIUMPH) at the University of Wisconsin School of Medicine and Public Health.

YARN BOMBING INSTRUCTIONS

Thanks to steward Eowyn Savela (page 126) for providing this tutorial for knitting your Little Free Library a sweater. For a smaller project, try yarn bombing only the post of your Little Library.

Yarn

- Use bulky or doubled-up worsted weight for a quick knit.
- This is the perfect time to use cheap acrylic yarn.
- Source yarn creatively:
  - Get it from the thrift shop.
  - Shop your own yarn stash for leftovers.
  - Ask your local knitting groups.
  - Put the call out to your Little Free Library patrons.

Needles

If you do use bulky yarn or doubled worsted, go for the big size 15 needles. This will make your knitting go super fast, and help create a nice, stretchy fabric (see Gauge).

Design and Construction

This is the fun part! Yarn bombs work well with bold designs and bright colors. Keep in mind that this is a temporary object, so keep things simple and save your intricate, time-intensive knitting for keepsakes.

Measure the dimensions of all the surfaces you'll be covering. Make your sweater narrower than your width measurements so that it has to stretch tightly around the Library (and won't sag down). Knit your Library sweater flat so that you can sew it into place around your Library. You can make a frame around the door with narrow strips of knitting. Go all out and cover the post, too!

Gauge

Usually yarn bombs work best when they are stretchy and they hug tight to the object they're wrapping. No matter which weight of yarn you use, knit a little more loosely than the recommended gauge so your knitted fabric has lots of stretch.

Installation

Wrap your Library in its cozy sweater (you may need an assistant). Stretch the sweater tight and sew it together around the Library. Your sweater will "wear

in" and stretch out over time, so keep it pretty tight to start with. Don't worry if it doesn't sit right after you finish sewing; you're going to fine-tune the fit next. Once you're done sewing, use a whole pile of little brass thumbtacks to secure the sweater to the Library and make it stay put in the right places.

What else?

- Make sure your Library is fully finished with paint or stain before you give it a sweater. Yarn doesn't keep the rain out.
- Your Library sweater is not permanent. It will get weathered and start to sag and look bad. That's how you'll know it's time to take it down . . . and make a new one!
- You could make your Library a new sweater for every season.
- Involve your Library patrons by asking them to knit squares for a patchwork sweater.
- Put together a learn-to-knit kit with needles, yarn, and basic knitting instructions. Offer it up in your Library to spread the knitting love.
- Have fun!

CALL FOR STORIES

*Do you have a story
to share about your
Little Free Library?
We'd love to
hear from you.*

Visit littlefreelibrary.org/steward-stories

ACKNOWLEDGMENTS

There have been thousands of people who've helped make a better world for all of us through the Little Free Library movement. First and foremost, we never would have gotten off the ground without the dedication and guidance of Rick Brooks. He has a keen mind for starting community engagement projects and was instrumental during some of our most difficult times. Even though Rick retired in April 2014, he continues to be a great supporter and promoter of Little Free Library.

My wife, Susan Bol, has often been referred to as the First Little Free Library Volunteer. My children, Allison and Austin, were also a huge help, always willing to paint, stain, build, stuff envelopes, and fix my computer whenever I needed them to.

Our dedicated staff members have worked for little or no pay at times, and always for far less than what they are worth. To Melissa Eystad, Jim Mercier, Kris Huson, Verna Clark, Elizabeth Kennedy, Megan Hanson, Branden Pedersen, Casey Dawson, Tony Bol, and Mark Alfuth, I extend my heartfelt gratitude and thanks.

We officially became a nonprofit on May 17, 2012. Since then, we've been fortunate to have an excellent board whose members receive no compensation whatsoever. They continually step up and guide our processes, structure, and development as we strive to become the best organization we can be to better serve our communities. Thank you Brian MacKenzie, Kristen Davis, Monnie McMahon, Jim Cosgrove, and Matt Ludt—their work is difficult and demanding, and they do it wholeheartedly.

We have a supporting cast of so many fans, friends, and stewards that it would take a separate book just to list them all. I can't thank all of you enough, especially Lisa Lopez, David Laufer, Eric and Victoria Miller, Linda Prout, the Prairie Du Chien Correctional Facility, Kathy Jordan, Sage Holben, Connie Goldman, Jan Hively, Sarah Brooks, and Brit Springer.

Thank you to the staff of Coffee House Press, particularly publisher Chris Fischbach. Coffee House has been with us from the beginning, donating thousands of free books to our stewards long before anyone else even knew who we were. Thanks also to Margret Aldrich, the teller of our tale; it has been the greatest of pleasures to work with a supporter who is so passionate and dedicated to sharing the Little Free Library story.

Little Free Library team leaders Melissa Eystad, Kris Huson, Mark Alfuth, and I always say that the real heart of this story lies in the individuals who freely share their love of books and communities every day. We and the rest of the Little Free Library staff feel so fortunate to represent all of them.

—Todd Bol

A book about community, creativity, and the kindness of strangers wouldn't be possible without a whole team of neighborly, creative, and kind people.

Thank you, first, to Todd Bol, Rick Brooks, Megan Hanson, and everyone at Little Free Library for their generosity in sharing their time and expertise to help this book reflect LFL's mission. Todd gets an extra shout-out for inviting my husband and me to build our very own Little Free Library alongside him at LFL Headquarters.

Thanks and gratitude to Chris Fischbach and Anitra Budd for inviting me to the table and to Caroline Casey, Linda Koutsky, Molly Fuller, Amelia Foster, and everyone at Coffee House Press for their ideas and dynamite talent.

Huge thanks to all of the Little Free Library stewards who shared their amazing stories (for every Little Library in the book, there are twenty more I wanted to include) and to Billy Collins, Nancy Pearl, Jay Walljasper, John McKnight, and Kelly Pajek for talking to me about the Little Libraries' appeal.

A special thank you to my Minneapolis neighbors who keep my Little Free Library hopping.

And, lastly, love and thanks to Gar, Abe, and Asher, the best Little Free Library spotters around.

—Margret Aldrich

PHOTO CREDITS

COVER (clockwise from left):
Charter number 194; steward: Linda Prout. Reprinted by permission.

Charter number 2621; stewards: Jennifer and Vernon Winters. Reprinted by permission.

Charter number 1; steward: Todd Bol. Reprinted by permission.

Charter number 5678; steward: Shawna Traver. Reprinted by permission of the steward and photographer Linda Koutsky.

Charter number 8001; steward: Glen Pangle. Reprinted by permission.

Charter number 4568; steward: Jennifer Pierce. Designed and built by Jeffrey Swainhart. Reprinted by permission of steward and photographer Linda Koutsky.

Photo reprinted by permission of the Decatur Book Festival. Photo by Jeff Stafford.

Charter number 7739; stewards: Jaimie and Sue Halliday. Reprinted by permission of the stewards and photographer Emily Tremel.

Charter number 10887; steward: Cotton Bryan. Reprinted by permission.

Charter number 3964; steward: Dr. Tariq Saleem Marwat. Reprinted by permission.

Charter number 5023; steward: David Gay. Reprinted by permission.

Charter number 12012; stewards: John Kieltyka and Monika Lidman. © John Kieltyka (www.verkstad. com). Reprinted by permission.

TITLE PAGE
(clockwise from top left):
Charter number 1309; steward: Walnut Way Conservation Group. Reprinted by permission.

Charter number 444 (two libraries); steward: Sarah Knoblauch. Reprinted by permission.

Charter number 7986; steward: Jeanne Carter. Reprinted by permission of Bird House Inn and photographer Linda Koutsky.

Charter number 5678; steward: Shawna Traver. Reprinted by permission of the steward and photographer Linda Koutsky.

Charter number 194; steward: Linda Prout. Reprinted by permission.

Charter unknown; steward: the American Swedish Institute. Reprinted by permission of steward and photographer Jon Dahlin.

Charter number 1; steward: Todd Bol. Reprinted by permission.

Charter number 2621; stewards: Jennifer and Vernon Winters. Reprinted by permission.

Charter number 4568; steward: Jennifer Pierce. Designed and built by Jeffrey Swainhart. Reprinted by permission of steward and photographer Linda Koutsky.

Charter number 2836; steward: Rachel Pennig. Reprinted by permission.

Charter number 3964; steward: Dr. Tariq Saleem Marwat. Reprinted by permission.

Charter number 10887; steward: Cotton Bryan. Reprinted by permission.

Charter number 4411; stewards: Dorothy and John Sweet. Reprinted by permission from the Bulletin/Central Oregon Living Magazine.

Charter number 12012; stewards: John Kieltyka and Monika Lidman. © John Kieltyka (www.verkstad. com). Reprinted by permission.

Charter number 287; steward: Kent Petterson. Reprinted by permission of photographer Linda Koutsky.

Charter numbers: multiple; steward: Sarah Maxey. Reprinted by permission.

Charter number 8001; steward: Glen Pangle. Reprinted by permission.

Charter number 0232; steward: Melody Moore. Reprinted by permission.

BOOK INTERIOR
Page v: Charter unknown; steward: the American Swedish Institute. Reprinted by permission of steward and photographer Jon Dahlin.

Pages vi–vii, 3, 31, and 250: Charter number 1; steward: Todd Bol. Reprinted by permission.

Page viii (left to right):
Charter number 12437; stewards: The Tarascio Family. Reprinted by Permission.

Charter number 2958; steward: Chad Stanton. Reprinted by permission of Little Free Library.

Charter number 2144; steward: Julie Eckert. Reprinted by permission of Little Free Library.

Charter number 5372; steward: Mary Smith. Reprinted by permission of Little Free Library.

Charter number 2410; steward: Amber Williams. Reprinted by permission

of Little Free Library.
Page 1: Charter number 2741;
steward: Pinehurst
Community Council.
Reprinted by permission of
Little Free Library.
Page 2: Charter number 4875;
steward: Rebecca Newland.
Reprinted by permission of
Little Free Library.
Page 5: photo of Lutie E. Stearns
(WHS-29372). Reprinted by
permission of the Wisconsin
Historical Society.
Page 6: Charter number 2224;
steward: Bassett Creek Arts.
Reprinted by permission of
Little Free Library.
Page 7, 43–45, and 222–223:
PEN World Voices and the
Architectural League of New
York.
   Designer: Cevan Castle
      Community Partner: The
      Clemente Soto Vélez
      Cultural and Educational
      Center
   Design Team: The Irwin S.
      Chanin School of
      Architecture's Design III
      studio with Maja Hjertén
      Knutson and Christopher
      Taleff, design leaders;
      Michael Young, David
      Allin, and Lydia Kallipoliti,
      faculty team
   Community Partner: The
      Cooper Union for the
      Advancement of Science
      and Architecture
   Design Team: Davies Tang +
      Toews
   Community Partner: La MaMa
   Design Team: Stereotank
   Community Partner: St.
      Patrick's Old Cathedral
      School and the They Co.
   Design Team: Shannon
      Harvey, Adam Michaels,
      and Levi Murphy
   Community Partner: Hester
      Street Collaborative
   Design Team: Forrest Jessee
      and Brigette Borders,

studio point 0
   Community Partner: Abrons
      Art Center/Henry Street
      Settlement
   Design Team: stpmj
   Community Partner: Fourth
      Arts Block
   Design Team: Matter
      Practice
   Community Partner: New
      York University
   Designer: Chat Travieso
   Community Partner: Two
      Bridges Neighborhood
      Council
   Design Team: Mark
      Rakatansky Studio with
      Aaron White
   Community Partner:
      University Settlement
Pages 8–9, 241, 251, and 263:
   Charter number 6879;
   steward: Margret Aldrich.
   Reprinted by permission of
   the steward and photogra-
   pher Nathan Kavlie (www.
   nathankavlie.com).
Page 10 (left to right):
   Charter number 11052;
      stewards: Kelly and Tim B.
      Reprinted by permission
      of Little Free Library.
   Charter number 1555;
      steward: Deborah Binder.
      Reprinted by permission
      of Little Free Library.
   Charter number 7309;
      steward: Maryanne
      Pacitti. Reprinted by
      permission of Little Free
      Library.
   Charter number 5390;
      steward: Judson Memorial
      Baptist Church. Reprinted
      by permission of Little
      Free Library.
   Charter number 5477;
      steward: Almantas Kulbis.
      Reprinted by permission
      of Little Free Library.
Page 11: Charter number 5003;
   steward: Kimberly Vowell.
   Reprinted by permission of
   Little Free Library.

Page 12: Charter number 7774;
   steward: Patty Tompkins.
   Reprinted by permission.
Pages 13: Charter number
   2621; stewards: Jennifer and
   Vernon Winters. Reprinted
   by permission.
Page 14: Charter number 3261;
   steward: Darlene Durfee.
   Reprinted by permission of
   Little Free Library.
Page 15 (top right): Charter
   number 15521; steward:
   Angela Wiseman. Reprinted
   by permission.
Page 15 (top left): Charter
   number 18679; steward:
   Camille Wilson. Reprinted
   by permission.
Page 15 (bottom center):
   Charter number 9112;
   stewards: Ken and Camille
   Goodwin. Reprinted by
   permission.
Page 15 (right): Charter
   number 14052; steward:
   Hilda Guerrero. Reprinted
   by permission of Little Free
   Library.
Page 16: Charter number
   17713; steward: Mindy
   Lubeck. Reprinted by
   permission of Little Free
   Library.
Page 17 (left): Charter number
   7453; steward: Rick
   Schroeder. Reprinted by
   permission.
Page 17 (right): Charter
   number 10278; steward:
   Elizabeth Faubert. Reprinted
   by permission of Little Free
   Library.
Page 18: Charter number 9581;
   steward: Rick C. Reprinted
   by permission of Little Free
   Library.
Page 19: Charter number 8785;
   steward: Diane B. Reprinted
   by permission of Little Free
   Library.
Pages 20–21: interview with
   Nancy Pearl. Reprinted by
   permission.

Page 21 (top): Charter number unknown; steward: unknown. Reprinted by permission of photographer Tara Gardner.

Page 21 (bottom): Charter number: 5689; steward: unknown. Reprinted by permission of photographer Tara Gardner.

Page 22: Charter number 7313; stewards: Alison Marti and Adam Margulies. Reprinted by permission of the stewards and photographer Tara Gardner.

Page 23 (top): Charter 10320; stewards Ann McKee and Dale Hoff. Built by Dale Hoff, Craftsman. This design and others available for purchase at www.handcraftsinwordandwood.com. Reprinted by permission of the stewards and photographer Tara Gardner.

Page 23 (bottom): Charter number 2572; stewards: Janine Firpo and Mike Taylor. Reprinted by permission of the stewards and photographer Tara Gardner.

Page 23 (margin from top to botttom):

Charter number 4512; steward: Allison Young. Reprinted by permission of the steward and photographer Tara Gardner.

Charter unknown. Reprinted by permission of photographer Tara Gardner.

Charter 4995; steward: Jackson Burger. Reprinted by permission of the steward and photographer Tara Gardner.

Charter Unknown. Reprinted by permission of photographer Tara Gardner.

Pages 24: Photo provided by Linda Koutsky. Reprinted by permission.

Page 26–27: Charter number 444; steward: Sarah Knoblauch. Reprinted by permission of steward and photographer Linda Koutsky.

Page 28 (left to right):

Charter number 2224; steward: Bassett Creek Arts. Reprinted by permission of Little Free Library.

Charter number 2679; steward: Kathy Rossol. Reprinted by permission of Little Free Library.

Charter number 11598; steward: Michelle McLaughlin. Reprinted by permission of Little Free Library.

Charter number 10975; steward: Nolan Middle School TSA Maureen Hudson. Reprinted by permission of Little Free Library.

Charter number 4170; steward: Gina Ruppert. Reprinted by permission of Little Free Library.

Page 29: Charter number 3031; steward: Rebecca Brenna. Reprinted by permission of Little Free Library.

Page 30: Charter number 5265; steward: Steve Fratoni. Reprinted by permission of Little Free Library.

Page 32: Charter number 14828; steward: Bob DeWit. Reprinted by permission of Little Free Library.

Page 33: Charter number 10164; steward: Swapna Krishna. Reprinted by permission. First published in Book Riot.

Page 34: Charter number 8363; steward: Karen V. Reprinted by permission of Little Free Library.

Page 35 (right): Charter number 19509; steward: Star Edwards. Reprinted by permission.

Page 35 (left): Charter number 6593; steward: Russell Riediger. Reprinted by permission of Little Free Library.

Pages 37–38: Charter number 1925; stewards: Finn, Ginny, and Kyle Pennekamp. Reprinted by permission.

Pages 39–40; Charter numbers: multiple; steward: Sarah Maxey. Reprinted by permission.

Pages 41–42: Charter number 4621; stewards: Khalid, Saad, Umayr, and Yasmin Ansari. Reprinted by permission.

Pages 46–47: Charter number 3570; steward: Mike Haeg. Reprinted by permission.

Page 48 (left): Charter number 14931; stewards: Noel/Kristen Mayeske. Reprinted by permission of Little Free Library.

Pages 48 (right)–49: Charter number 7864; steward: James Copeland. Reprinted by permission.

Pages 50–51: Charter number 3254; steward: Carolyn Bancroft. Reprinted by permission.

Pages 52–53: Charter numbers: 7749, 9452, and 10045; steward: DooSun You. Reprinted by permission.

Page 54: Charter number 7559; steward: Debe Edden. Reprinted by permission.

Pages 55 and 57: Charter number 4840; stewards: Ellen and Col Cseke. Reprinted by permission of the stewards and Diane + Mike Photography.

Page 58: Charter number 4868; stewards: Beth and Brian Cason. Reprinted by

permission of Little Free Library.

Page 59 (top and bottom): Photos from the Little Free Library workshop. Photos by Margret Aldrich and Todd Bol. Reprinted by permission.

Page 59 (right): Charter number 14415; steward: Angelica Gonzalez. Reprinted by permission of Little Free Library.

Page 60–61: Charter number 4455; stewards: Maggie Moris and Kent Kokko. Reprinted by permission of stewards and photographer Linda Koutsky.

Page 62 (left to right): Charter number 10769; steward: Nicole Bellmore Pierse. Reprinted by permission of Little Free Library.

Charter number 2259; steward: Colete Grubman. Reprinted by permission of Little Free Library.

Charter number 4842; steward: Jennifer Brozek. Reprinted by permission of Little Free Library.

Charter number 7817; steward: Laurie Marks. Reprinted by permission of Little Free Library.

Charter number 11534; steward: Rachel Rury. Reprinted by permission of Little Free Library.

Page 63: Charter number 16336; steward: Vigo County Public Library. Reprinted by permission of Little Free Library.

Page 64: Charter number 7830; steward: Melanie Peterson-Nafziger. Reprinted by permission.

Page 66 (right and left): Charter number 5897; stewards: Meleah Maynard

and Mike Hoium. Reprinted by permission.

Pages 67–69: Charter number 10887; steward: Cotton Bryan. Reprinted by permission.

Pages 71: Charter number 4932; steward: Lieke Ploeger. Reprinted by permission.

Page 72: Little Free Library Original. Reprinted by permission of Little Free Library.

Page 73: Charter number 4918; steward: Sally Harris. Reprinted by permission of Little Free Library.

Page 74: Charter numbers: multiple. Reprinted by permission of Little Brothers—Friends of the Elderly, Minneapolis/St. Paul Chapter LuAnne Speeter. Reprinted by permission.

Page 75: Charter number 10581; steward: Frank M. Reprinted by permission of Little Free Library.

Pages 76–77: Charter number 7524; stewards: Amy Walton and James Garrett. Reprinted by permission.

Page 78 (left): Charter number 3160; stewards: Barbara and Thomas Dorn. Reprinted by permission of Little Free Library.

Page 78 (right): Charter number 7504; steward: Pat Pobst. Reprinted by permission.

Page 79 (left): Charter number 1612; steward: Susan Reep. Reprinted by permission.

Page 79: (right) Charter number 4204; steward: Charlie Kenny. Reprinted by permission of Little Free Library.

Page 80: Charter number 14060; steward: Bev Peaslee. Reprinted by permission of Little Free

Library.

Page 81: Charter number 2896; steward: Larissa Kyzer. Reprinted by permission.

Page 83: Charter number 7078; steward: Harlem Grown. Reprinted by permission.

Page 85: Charter number 10883; stewards: Chris and Rosalie Street. Reprinted by permission.

Page 86 (top): Charter number 15372; steward: Caramel Quin. Reprinted by permission of Little Free Library.

Page 86 (bottom): Charter number 14675; steward: Matilda Sodderland. Reprinted by permission of Little Free Library.

Pages 87–89: interview with Jay Walljasper. Reprinted by permission.

Page 88 (left to right): Charter number 3747; steward: Dean Bonner. Reprinted by permission of Little Free Library.

Charter number 5938; steward: Carrie Burdzinski. Reprinted by permission of Little Free Library.

Charter number 8495; steward: Connie Hazeltine. Reprinted by permission of Little Free Library.

Charter number 12141; stewards: Christian and Tiffany H. Reprinted by permission of Little Free Library.

Charter number 3962; steward: Jennifer Stieren. Reprinted by permission of Little Free Library.

Page 89 (left to right): Charter number 2570; steward: Lester Strom. Reprinted by permission of Little Free Library.

Charter number 3744;

stewards: Jay MacBride & Emily Ronning. Reprinted by permission of Little Free Library.

Charter number 14943; steward: Mike VanDan. Reprinted by permission of Little Free Library.

Charter number 2997; steward: Ann Engleman. Reprinted by permission of Little Free Library.

Charter number 13629; steward: Rob W. Reprinted by permission of Little Free Library.

Page 90–91: Charter number 568; steward: Jim Kroupa. Reprinted by permission of steward and photographer Linda Koutsky.

Page 92 (left to right):
Charter number 12151; steward: Theresa Perales. Reprinted by permission of Little Free Library.

Charter number 8747; steward: Suzanne Janse-Vreeling. Reprinted by permission.

Charter number 7751; steward: Helena Paulen. Reprinted by permission of Little Free Library.

Charter number 8351; steward: Nancy Lindquist. Reprinted by permission of Little Free Library.

Charter number 6899; steward: Chris Orr. Reprinted by permission of Little Free Library.

Page 93: Charter number 18538; steward: Dale Rupright. Reprinted by permission of Little Free Library.

Pages 95–96: Charter number 9398; steward: Carolyn Williams-Noren. This Little Free Library (the Little Poetry Library) was created by a fiscal year 2013 recipient of an Artist

Initiative grant from the Minnesota State Arts Board. This activity is made possible by the voters of Minnesota through a grant from the Minnesota State Arts Board, thanks to a legislative appropriation from the arts and cultural heritage fund. Reprinted by permission.

Pages 97–98: Charter number 20193; stewards: 826LA. Additional photos provided by 826LA. Reprinted by permission.

Pages 99–101: text by Jocelyn Hale, executive director of the Loft Literary Center. Reprinted by permission.

Page 100: Charter number 1505; steward: Jocelyn Hale. Reprinted by permission of the steward and photographer Theodore Miller.

Page 101: Charter number 5370; steward: Elizabeth Maltby. Reprinted by permission of Little Free Library.

Page 102: Charter number 4939; steward: Marianne Fellner. Reprinted by permission of Little Free Library.

Page 103 (left): Charter number 8761; steward: John Sellers. Reprinted by permission.

Page 103 (right): Charter number 2893; stewards: Randy & Collen Conner-Renaye. Reprinted by permission of Little Free Library.

Pages 105–106: Charter numbers: multiple; steward: Evgenia Pirog. Reprinted by permission.

Pages 107–108 and endsheets: Charter number 6315; stewards: David Strange and Nancy Vogl. Reprinted by permission of the stewards and Emilee Machelle

Photography.

Pages 109–111: Charter numbers: multiple. Reprinted by permission of the Type Rider II Poetry Tour (Maya Stein and Amy Tingle). Photos by Stephanie Renee.

Page 112: Charter number 14684; steward: Stacy Dickert-Conlin. Reprinted by permission of Little Free Library.

Page 113: Steward: Northrop Urban Environmental Learning Center. Reprinted by permission of the Minneapolis Public Schools.

Pages 114–115: Charter numbers: multiple. Reprinted by permission of the Decatur Book Festival. Photo by Jeff Stafford.

Pages 116–117 and 119: Charter numbers: multiple; steward: Lisa Lopez. Reprinted by permission.

Page 118: Charter number 1147; steward: Elizabeth Andrews. Reprinted by permission of Little Free Library.

Page 120 (right): Charter number 9440; steward: Lilian Negron. Reprinted by permission.

Page 120 (left) Charter number 15365; steward: Suzanne Scheuerman. Reprinted by permission of Little Free Library.

Pages 121, 206–208, and 218 (right): Charter numbers: multiple. Photos provided by Foster the Future (fosterthe-future.com). Reprinted by permission of Foster the Future.

Page 121 (right): Charter number 6938; steward: Wanda White. Reprinted by permission of Little Free Library.

Pages 122–123 and 141:

Charter number 5017; steward: Kathy Ross. Reprinted by permission.

Page 124 (left to right): Charter number 7997; steward: Jennifer Pennington. Reprinted by permission of Little Free Library.

Charter number 5843; steward: Evette S. Reprinted by permission of Little Free Library.

Charter number 12843; steward: Joy N. Reprinted by permission of Little Free Library.

Charter number 12147; steward: Julie Turgeon. Reprinted by permission of Little Free Library.

Charter number 4455; steward: Maggie Moris. Reprinted by permission.

Page 125: Charter number 6071; steward: Laurie Miller. Reprinted by permission of Little Free Library.

Pages 126–127: Charter number 4411; stewards: Dorothy and John Sweet. Reprinted by permission from the Bulletin/Central Oregon Living Magazine.

Pages 128–129 and 247–248: Charter number 11105; stewards: Eowyn and Jesse Savela. Yarn bombing instructions by Eowyn Savela. Reprinted by permission.

Pages 130–131: Charter number 7082; steward: Karri Folks. Reprinted by permission.

Pages 132–133: Charter number 4048; stewards: Kirk Brust and Maria Olsen. Reprinted by permission.

Page 135: Charter number 7739; stewards: Jaimie and Sue Halliday. Reprinted by permission of the stewards and photographer Emily Tremel.

Pages 137 and 214–215: Charter number 4944; steward: Peter Homan and Christine Waslander. Reprinted by permission.

Page 138: text by Billy Collins. Reprinted by permission.

Page 138: Charter number 0232; steward: Melody Moore. Reprinted by permission.

Page 139: photographs and sculpture by Doug Senalik. Reprinted by permission.

Page 143: Charter number 8297; steward: Kieran Leopold. Reprinted by permission.

Pages 145 and 167 (left): Charter number 1955; steward: Tracy Mumford. Reprinted by permission of the steward and photographer Asher Miller.

Page 147: illustrations by Mary Katherine Buike. Reprinted by permission of MKBuike/Red Harp Arts (redharparts.worpress.com).

Page 149: Charter number 9391; stewards: Louie and Missy Feher-Peiker and Diane and Jim Peiker. Reprinted by permission.

Page 150: Charter number 4414; steward: Theresa B. Reprinted by permission of Little Free Library.

Page 151 (right): Charter number 4672; steward: Kathi Titus. Reprinted by permission of Little Free Library.

Page 151 (left) and 253: Charter number 5805; steward: Beth Perry. Reprinted by permission.

Pages 152–153: Charter number 5403; steward: Delia Cosentino. Reprinted by permission.

Page 154 (left to right): Charter number 3583; steward: Robin Cox. Reprinted by permission of Little Free Library.

Charter number 9664; stewards: Martha and Brent K. Reprinted by permission of Little Free Library.

Charter number 4588; steward: MaryLee S. Reprinted by permission of Little Free Library.

Charter number 13520; steward: Marge I. Reprinted by permission of Little Free Library.

Page 155: Charter number 10380; steward: Debby F. Reprinted by permission of Little Free Library.

Page 156: Illustration by Bill Whitehead. Reprinted by permission.

Page 157: Charter number 11848; stewards: Brian, Sarah, and Spencer Collins. Reprinted by permission.

Page 158: Charter number 7199; steward: Shana Bregenzer-Brenny. Reprinted by permission of Little Free Library.

Page 159 (right): Charter number 9792; steward: Lissa Wagner. Reprinted by permission of Little Free Library.

Page 159 (top and bottom): Charter number 4996; steward: Jeanne Ratzloff. Reprinted by permission.

Page 161: Charter number 6357; steward: David Carr. Reprinted by permission.

Pages 163 and 165: Charter number 6767; stewards: Naomi, Sarah, Scott, and Stacey Porter. Reprinted by permission.

Page 166: Charter number 4842; steward: Jennifer Brozek. Reprinted by permission of Little Free Library.

Page 167 (right): Charter number 4937; steward: Tommy Marshall. Reprinted by permission of Little Free Library.

Page 168: Charter number 2679; steward: Geneva Village Homemakers. Reprinted by permission of Little Free Library.

Pages 169–170: Charter numbers: multiple. Photos provided by the Los Angeles Police Department. Reprinted by permission.

Page 171–172: Charter numbers: multiple; steward: Carrizozo Works, Inc. Reprinted by permission.

Page 173 (right): Charter number 12376; steward: Barbara McDonald. Reprinted by permission of Little Free Library.

Page 175: Charter number 4764; stewards: Christine Mihok and Tara Ryan, Hope for Highlands. Reprinted by permission.

Page 176: Charter number 12012; stewards: John Kieltyka and Monika Lidman. © John Kieltyka (www. verkstad.com). Reprinted by permission.

Page 177: Charter number 11331; stewards: Karen and Bob White. © John Kieltyka (www.verkstad.com). Reprinted by permission of the stewards and photographer John Kieltyka.

Page 178: Charter number 6470; steward: Cleveland Neighborhood. Reprinted by permission of Little Free Library.

Page 179 (left): Charter number 12437; stewards: The Tarascio Family. Reprinted by permission.

Page 179 (right): Charter number 3899; steward: Jessica Eckstrom. Reprinted

by permission of Little Free Library.

Page 180–181: Charter number 2393; steward; Tom Moffatt. Designed by local sculptor Aaron Dysart. Reprinted by permission of the steward and photographer Linda Koutsky.

Page 182 (left to right): Charter number 1829; steward: Tammy Cook. Reprinted by permission of Little Free Library. Charter number 7200; steward: Samuel Jandt. Reprinted by permission of Little Free Library. Charter number 2355; steward: Julie Lowe. Reprinted by permission of Little Free Library. Charter number 9346; steward: Marylee P. Reprinted by permission of Little Free Library. Charter number 3016; stewards: Joanne Esser and Mike Hay. Reprinted by permission of Little Free Library.

Page 183: Charter number 1097; steward: Liz Reiser. Reprinted by permission of Little Free Library.

Pages 184–185: Charter numbers: multiple. Photos provided by Dr. Jonathan Dickman and the TRaining In Urban Medicine and Public Health (TRIUMPH) program at the University of Wisconsin School of Medicine and Public Health.

Page 186: Charter number 5137; stewards: Paul and Oceana Seer. Reprinted by permission of Little Free Library.

Page 187: Charter number 16307; steward: Jennifer Albers. Reprinted by permission of Little Free Library.

Pages 189: Charter numbers: multiple. Photo provided by Lisa Heydlauff and Going to School. Reprinted by permission.

Pages 191–195 Charter numbers: multiple; steward: Linda Prout. Reprinted by permission.

Page 196: Charter number 2056; steward: Tina Sipula. Reprinted by permission.

Page 199: Charter number 260; stewards: Helen Crary Stassen and Jay Stassen, whose contribution is made in loving memory of their son, Benjamin Curry Stassen. Reprinted by permission.

Page 201: Charter numbers: multiple. Reprinted by permission of Books of Africa.

Pages 202–203: Charter numbers: multiple; steward: Dr. Tariq Saleem Marwat. Reprinted by permission.

Page 205: Charter number 5581; steward: Maria Gallegos. Reprinted by permission.

Page 209: Charter number 17899; steward: Kathy Ireland. Reprinted by permission of Little Free Library.

Pages 211–213: Charter numbers: multiple; steward: Kimberly Daugherty. Reprinted by permission.

Page 216 (left to right): Charter number 13629; steward: Rob W. Reprinted by permission of Little Free Library. Charter number 2002; stewards: Ray and Barbara Williamson. Reprinted by permission of Little Free Library. Charter number 16138; steward: Kim Waltman. Reprinted by permission of Little Free Library.

Charter number 14457; steward: Dave Clem. Reprinted by permission of Little Free Library.

Charter number unknown, steward: unknown. Reprinted by permission of Little Free Library.

Page 217: Charter number 8273; steward: Heidi Boyum. Reprinted by permission of Little Free Library.

Page 218 (left): Charter number 5404; steward: Leslie McDonough. Reprinted by permission of Little Free Library.

Page 219: Charter number 4625; steward: Amanda Bloom. Reprinted by permission of Little Free Library.

Page 220 (top): Charter number 5612; steward: Grace David. Reprinted by permission.

Page 220 (left): Charter number 13936; steward: Cindy Koesster. Reprinted by permission of Little Free Library.

Page 221: Charter number 19693; steward: Renee Flager. Reprinted by

permission of Little Free Library.

Pages 225–238: The plans for this version of the Little Free Library were designed by Paul Meisel and are reproduced with permission. You can purchase additional copies of this plan, as well as the required hardware from Meisel Hardware Specialties, P.O. Box 70, Mound, MN 55364, 800-441-9870 (www. meiselwoodhobby.com). Photos provided Paul Meisel.

Page 244: door counter tutorial and photo by Viel Catig. Reprinted by permission.

Pages 244–246: door counter tutorial and photos by Jonathan Dickman. Permission to use this tutorial was given by Jonathan Dickman, MD, PhD. This work was completed while Dr. Dickman was a medical student in the TRaining In Urban Medicine and Public Health (TRIUMPH) at the University of Wisconsin School of Medicine and Public Health.

Page 249: Charter number

20332; stewards Ali and Patrick Lee-O'Halloran. Reprinted by permission of the steward and photographer Laurie Haycraft/Dave Wogsland.

Page 254: Charter number 1728; steward: Calgary Reads. Reprinted by permission of Little Free Library.

Page 257: Charter number 17025; steward: Randi Nathanson. Reprinted by permission of Little Free Library.

Page 258: Charter number 13541; steward: Kay Torre. Reprinted by permission of Little Free Library.

Page 261: Charter number 13314; steward: Peter F. Reprinted by permission of Little Free Library.

BACK COVER:

(left) Charter number 7986; steward: Jeanne Carter. Reprinted by permission of Bird House Inn and photographer Linda Koutsky.

(right) Charter number 2836; steward: Rachel Pennig. Reprinted by permission.

Books in Action is an initiative by Coffee House Press to publish works and develop programs that encourage and nurture literary arts beyond the page, highlighting people and organizations working to further interdisciplinary collaborations, reader engagement, and nontraditional means of accessing the reading experience. For more information, please visit coffeehousepress.org/books-in-action.

OTHER BOOKS IN ACTION TITLES

Read This! Edited by Hans Weyandt
978-1-56689-313-8 • $12.00

The Artist's Library Erinn Batykefer and Laura Damon-Moore
978-1-56689-353-4 • $23.95

FUNDER ACKNOWLEDGMENTS

Coffee House Press is an independent, nonprofit literary publisher. All of our books, including the one in your hands, are made possible through the generous support of grants and donations from corporate giving programs, state and federal support, family foundations, and the many individuals that believe in the transformational power of literature. We receive major operating support from Amazon, the Bush Foundation, the McKnight Foundation, and Target. This activity is made possible by the voters of Minnesota through a Minnesota State Arts Board Operating Support grant, thanks to a legislative appropriation from the arts and cultural heritage fund. Our publishing program is also supported in part by the Jerome Foundation and an award from the National Endowment for the Arts. To find out more about how NEA grants impact individuals and communities, visit www.arts.gov.

Coffee House Press receives additional support from many anonymous donors; the Alexander Family Fund; the Archer Bondarenko Munificence Fund; the Elmer L. & Eleanor J. Andersen Foundation; the David & Mary Anderson Family Foundation; the E. Thomas Binger & Rebecca Rand Fund of the Minneapolis Foundation; the Patrick & Aimee Butler Family Foundation; the Buuck Family Foundation; the Carolyn Foundation; Dorsey & Whitney Foundation; Fredrikson & Byron, P.A.; the Lenfestey Family Foundation; the Mead Witter Foundation; the Rehael Fund of the Minneapolis Foundation; the Schwab Charitable Fund; Schwegman, Lundberg & Woessner, P.A.; Penguin Group; the Private Client Reserve of US Bank; VSA Minnesota for the Metropolitan Regional Arts Council; the Archie D. & Bertha H. Walker Foundation; the Wells Fargo Foundation of Minnesota; and the Woessner Freeman Family Foundation.

THE PUBLISHER'S CIRCLE OF COFFEE HOUSE PRESS

Publisher's Circle members make significant contributions to Coffee House Press's annual giving campaign. Understanding that a strong financial base is necessary for the press to meet the challenges and opportunities that arise each year, this group plays a crucial part in the success of our mission.

"Coffee House Press believes that American literature should be as diverse as America itself. Known for consistently championing authors whose work challenges cultural and aesthetic norms, we believe their books deserve space in the marketplace of ideas. Publishing literature has never been an easy business, and publishing literature that truly takes risks is a cause we believe is worthy of significant support. We ask you to join us today in helping to ensure the future of Coffee House Press."

—THE PUBLISHER'S CIRCLE MEMBERS OF COFFEE HOUSE PRESS

PUBLISHER'S CIRCLE MEMBERS INCLUDE

Many anonymous donors, Mr. & Mrs. Rand L. Alexander, Suzanne Allen, Patricia Beithon, Bill Berkson & Connie Lewallen, Robert & Gail Buuck, Claire Casey, Louise Copeland, Jane Dalrymple-Hollo, Mary Ebert & Paul Stembler, Chris Fischbach & Katie Dublinski, Katharine Freeman, Sally French, Jocelyn Hale & Glenn Miller, Roger Hale & Nor Hall, Jeffrey Hom, Kenneth & Susan Kahn, Kenneth Koch Literary Estate, Stephen & Isabel Keating, Allan & Cinda Kornblum, Leslie Larson Maheras, Jim & Susan Lenfestey, Sarah Lutman & Rob Rudolph, Carol & Aaron Mack, George Mack, Joshua Mack, Gillian McCain, Mary & Malcolm McDermid, Sjur Midness & Briar Andresen, Peter Nelson & Jennifer Swenson, Marc Porter & James Hennessy, E. Thomas Binger & Rebecca Rand Fund of the Minneapolis Foundation, Jeffrey Sugerman & Sarah Schultz, Nan Swid, Patricia Tilton, Stu Wilson & Melissa Barker, Warren D. Woessner & Iris C. Freeman, and Margaret & Angus Wurtele.

For more information about the Publisher's Circle and other ways to support Coffee House Press books, authors, and activities, please visit www.coffeehousepress.org/support or contact us at: info@coffeehousepress.org.

COFFEE HOUSE PRESS

The mission of Coffee House Press is to publish exciting, vital, and enduring authors of our time; to delight and inspire readers; to contribute to the cultural life of our community; and to enrich our literary heritage. By building on the best traditions of publishing and the book arts, we produce books that celebrate imagination, innovation in the craft of writing, and the many authentic voices of the American experience.

LITERATURE
is not the same thing as
PUBLISHING

Visit us at coffeehousepress.org

Margret Aldrich is a writer and editor who has published her work with the *Atlantic; Experience Life; Brain, Child;* and others. A former editor at *Utne Reader,* Margret is a regular contributor to *Book Riot* and is a producer at BringMeTheNews's national health platform. She lives in Minneapolis with her bearded husband, two entertaining young boys, and a Little Free Library.

THE MYSTERIOUS DISAPPEARANCE OF LEON · NEAR MURO

Ida B · GREENWILLOW

The Invisible Rules of the Zoë Lama · Dutton

...te's Web · E.B.White

Ruby Parker Hits the Small Time

Umbrella Summer

Library Rules: LOAN POLICY: Sit and Read, or Borro...

Lobel · Steig · Jackson/Simmons · SAILEY · STEVENS · Emsley Cheung · Gilhuin · McGuire · LITTLE YELLOW PEAR TOMATOES · Hansel and Gretel

Sylvester and the Magic Pebble · MY TALL BOOK OF THREE LITTLE PIGS · EPOSSUMONDAS PLAYS POSSUM · I Want You to Know: The Wonder of God · LaVon Bridges and Alice Wright · Alaska Animals We Love You · The Sky of Afghanistan · Ana A. de Eulate · Sonja Wimmer

THE TROLL MUSIC · VIOLET AND WINSTON · Simon & Schuster · PRESCHOOL PRESS